Summer of The Spotted Horse

by

Nancy Sanderson

authorHOUSE

1663 LIBERTY DRIVE, SUITE 200
BLOOMINGTON, INDIANA 47403
(800) 839-8640
www.authorhouse.com

This book is a work of fiction. Places, events, and situations in this story are purely fictional. Any resemblance to actual persons, living or dead, is coincidental.

First published by AuthorHouse 05/14/04

ISBN: 1-4184-1317-8. (sc)

Printed in the United States of America
Bloomington, IN

This book is printed on acid free paper.

For Mom and Dad

Table of Contents

ACKNOWLEDGMENTS

Special thanks to my friend, Terry, a middle school librarian and former race trainer and owner who checked the manuscript for authenticity; also my aunts, Kelly and Edie, lifelong readers, who read the story and offered positive comments; my sister, Bonnie, and my brother, Paul, for their enthusiasm and support. And to my husband, Tom, who helps me edit and patiently puts up with a wife who either has her head stuck in a book or is pounding away on a laptop.

The Sport of Kings

Our newly-born foal wobbles to his feet,
And greets his gentle mama with a tiny whinny.
She reassures him with a throaty nicker,
And tenderly nuzzles his small, wet nose.

He doesn't know it yet, but his destiny is one of glory,
For his sire is King of the turf,
And his lovely dam, a princess of the blood.
Soon, it will be his time to reign.

We watch him as he grows.
Will the rest of him ever fit those legs?
He tosses his head and streaks across the pasture. Who
cares!

Suddenly, the great adventure begins.
Eyes shiny, we watch him as he dances on tippy-toes
Down the track, answering the call to post.
"The flag is up! And there they go!"

The crowd murmurs in excitement,
For they, too, have bought a piece of the magic.
As the horses round the far turn, the hum grows louder,
Until we can no longer hear them.

We can feel them, though, pounding down the stretch,
The earth trembling beneath their mighty hoofs.
We can feel it starting in our toes and rushing up through
our whole bodies,
Exploding in a hoarse yell, as our colt crosses the wire!

Chapter I

WHERE'S MY DAD?

Sixteen-year-old Samantha Kelly was ticked. In fact, she couldn't remember when she had ever been more ticked in her life, except maybe last week when she'd seen Kevin Murray out riding with Tiffany Miller – the same Kevin Murray who was supposed to be *her* boyfriend. *Forget about that. I'm going to be much too busy working my horse at the racetrack this summer to think about boys anyway.*

With a huge sigh of relief, she glimpsed the top of a Ferris wheel through an avenue of oak trees on her right. At last, her destination was in sight.

"You'd think that after I suffer through a boring, nine-hour bus ride from San Bernardino, someone would at least meet me at the station," she grumbled as the taxi stopped in front of the horsemen's gate at the fairgrounds in Pleasanton.

Sliding out of the back seat, she fished a crumpled five-dollar bill from the pocket of her Levi jacket and handed it to the driver. Her backpack slipped down her arm, and she hiked it back up onto her shoulder with a groan. It had seemed a whole lot lighter earlier in the day.

"You want some change, little lady?" the cab driver asked pleasantly as he handed her a battered paisley suitcase. She found his cheerful voice especially irritating, and the gloomy gray skies did nothing to brighten her mood.

"Keep it," she grouched, grabbing the bag and storming off toward the gate. Her conscience made her turn back to apologize, but the driver had already left. "Oh, man," she mumbled under her breath, more frustrated than ever.

"Hey, Sam, welcome back," said the friendly gate guard as she walked quickly past him and flashed her racetrack I.D. "Your dad's trailer is in his regular spot over on row three."

"Thanks, Dewey," said Samantha, giving him a half-hearted smile and stuffing the card unceremoniously into her back pocket.

As she started for the horsemen's RV park, the guard called after her. "But he ain't there."

"What?" The girl slammed to a halt, pushed the brim of her baseball cap up and turned toward the guard, her hand on her hip. At this point, she'd just about had it.

"Well, where the heck is he, anyway?"

"Hold on there, missy," he scolded. "Don't go getting all mad at me."

"Sorry, Dewey. I'm just really tired, and I thought he'd be at the bus station. That's all."

"Well, your dad got hisself in some trouble over the weekend," the guard offered. He seemed embarrassed to have to give her this news. "No one's seen him since."

"Is Uncle Jack here?" the girl asked with new concern in her voice.

"Yeah, far as I know," was the reply. Samantha thanked him and turned back toward the RV park, wondering just what was going on.

As she expected, the backside was pretty much deserted since most of the horsemen were over at the racetrack this time of day. In fact, she didn't see a soul until an old cowboy with a gray beard waved his cane briefly at her from down the gravel drive. He was wearing dark glasses, and she didn't recognize him, but she waved back politely as she watched him limp away. *Wonder who that was? And why the shades on such a cloudy day?* She shrugged and continued toward her father's space. *Must be one of Dad's old buddies I haven't seen for awhile.*

Her mood brightened somewhat, and she walked a little faster when she spotted her best racetrack friend, Tracy Wilson, up ahead. The girl was sitting at the picnic table in front of her family's motor home, polishing a leather halter with neats-foot oil. *Well, at least somebody I know is here.*

"Hey, Trace," Samantha called. She hadn't seen Tracy since racing season ended last October and the trainers and their families had gone home for the winter. Tracy had been her summer best friend since they were ten, and she was anxious to compare notes about what had happened to each of them over the winter. They had e-mailed each other from time to time, but it wasn't the same as good old-fashioned side-by-side girl talk. She walked faster.

"Hi, Sam," the girl answered cheerfully. "Good to see you." Then her expression turned suddenly serious. She put the halter down and looked up as Samantha approached. "Actually, I'm kind of surprised to see you back, what with the trouble and all."

Samantha was just about to ask her about the "trouble" when Tracy's mother appeared at the door.

"Tracy! Inside now!" Mrs. Wilson commanded. Tracy rolled her eyes up and shrugged. Then, she picked up the halter and went inside. When she turned to say good-bye to her friend, her mother

4

practically slammed the door in Samantha's face. She was shocked and a little dismayed, and she could feel her cheeks turning hot and red. No one had ever slammed a door in her face before today. Then she shrugged and headed for her father's trailer.

Well, that's weird. Dad's disappeared, and my best friend's mother won't let her talk to me. What's that all about anyway?

Spotting her father's big fifth-wheeler, Samantha was relieved to find that at least she had a place to stay. She dropped her suitcase and backpack on the table out front and tried the door. It was locked. She felt under the mat for the spare key. No luck. She was mad all over again.

"Stupid thing!" she snapped, kicking the door. The metal twanged as she flopped down hard on the little doorstep, her elbows on her knees, her chin in her hands. A slight breeze blew a wisp of curly brown hair into her face, and she puffed up at it out of the corner of her mouth. She hoped her Uncle Jack would show up soon. It looked like it might rain.

Frustrated and disheartened, she got up and rummaged through her backpack for a pen and some paper. That was Samantha. Whenever she was really, really happy or really, really sad, she would sit down and write poetry. Writing verse would either make her much happier or take the edge off her sadness

– or make long, dreary bus rides less boring. She had been writing during most of the trip north. The new poem, "The Sport of Kings," was coming along pretty well. It just needed a little polishing.

Actually when she thought about it, she knew her talent for poetry came naturally. All the Malones were rhymers, from her mother, Ann, to Uncle Jack, to all of their sisters and brothers. They loved poetry – reading it, writing it and reciting it. And when they weren't spouting poems, they were singing because, after all, songs were poetry too. Her mother always said it was an Irish thing.

Although Samantha didn't think she'd ever be as talented as her mother, she had written some things she thought were pretty good. Lately, she had been trying unrhymed verse. When the class had gotten their English papers back the last day of school, she'd received an "A" on an unrhymed poem about her favorite subject, horses. She smiled a little when she remembered how surprised her friends had been when she first let them read some of her poems last year.

She was Sam, a little tough and tomboyish, who rode horses and was the star pitcher on the girls' softball team. She lived in Levis and tee shirts and wore her hair in a single braid that hung halfway down her back. Makeup was reserved for special occasions.

With what she called "her wild Irish nose" and blue-green eyes that turned slightly upwards at the corners, Samantha didn't consider herself movie star material. People called her "cute" and "perky," but no one had ever told her she was beautiful. She didn't dwell on it anyhow. Instead, she concentrated on finding the beauty in her world and trying to express it in her poetry. In sharing these personal thoughts, Samantha had, somewhat reluctantly at first, allowed others a glimpse of a softer side of her they hadn't ever known—the beauty that was in her heart.

Unfortunately, today wasn't going to be a poetry day. Samantha couldn't find any unused paper, and her only pen had disappeared. *Maybe poetry doesn't work on mad.*

Glumly, she looked around at the familiar surroundings of the Alameda County Fair where she had spent a happy two weeks of every summer for as long as she could remember. The RV park was neat and tidy, with big shady oak trees, redwood picnic tables and barbecue grills at every space.

A gravel driveway meandered around the park past campers, trailers and motor homes of every age, size and description. This part of the fairgrounds was not open to the public and was a refuge where trainers and their families could get away from the hustle and bustle of the racetrack for a while in the evenings after the last race was run. They could forget about angry bettors calling them names, and horses that didn't run as well as expected, and cocky jockeys who didn't ride as they were instructed.

Sometimes Samantha had to wonder why the horsemen came back year after year, but she knew that even after a dozen losses, it only took one big win to put them back on top of the world. In the heady excitement of watching your horse cross the wire first, you forgot the bad times in a heartbeat.

She had mostly pleasant memories of all the people she had gotten to know at the fairgrounds throughout California over the years. The fair circuit folk were like a little movable city that went from track to track during the summer months. When the two-week race meet was over at one fair, they all moved on to the next track – horses, houses and humans – all pulling up stakes and traveling on with the other big "H" – hope. They hoped the weather would hold, and they hoped their horses would stay healthy, and they hoped for enough wins to keep them going to the next fair.

Always, at the next meet, they might win "giant" and collect enough purse money to buy a little ranch out in the country where they could take life easy. But even when they won enough to buy a small spread, some of the race trackers like her father just couldn't quit. It was in their blood, and every year come spring, they'd just get restless.

"Annie, I gotta go just one more year," Frank Kelly would say to his wife. "Can't trust this colt (or filly or gelding) to anybody else."

Ann would shrug and say, "fine," and patiently pack his clothes. For her, the gypsy racetrack life had ended when Samantha's brother, James, was born. She had never regretted leaving the track, even when it meant running the ranch alone over the summer while her husband went racing.

After buying a small dairy farm, Grandpa Kelly, had never gone back to training at the track either. These days, he preferred his black and white Holstein cows to horses. He said they gave him a return on his money every day, unlike those "hay burners" who could take a misstep and put you out of business for a whole season. He did, however, have a wealth of knowledge about horses and was always willing to advise his son when a problem came up that Frank couldn't solve. Those kinds of problems were actually pretty rare, as Frank had practically been raised at the track while his father was training Thoroughbreds. He had learned the ins and outs of horse racing at his father's knee, and he still loved every minute of it.

So, every spring, like birds heading north for the summer, Frank and his brother-in-law would load up the big horse trailer, kiss the family good-bye and head out. Frank trailered the horses, and Uncle Jack drove the diesel pickup hauling the fifth-wheel trailer the two men would live in during the racing season.

From the time she was five, Samantha knew somehow that racing was in her blood too and begged to go along every year. Twice, they had discovered her hidden in the trailer, hoping they wouldn't find her until it was too late to turn back. Finally, the summer she was eight, she had "gone racing" for a couple of weeks. By the time she was ten, she was allowed to stay the whole summer.

She made herself useful, helping with the household and "horsehold" chores, as she called them. She worked hard like all the other horsemen's kids. They mucked out stalls and hauled feed and groomed horses, but they had time for play too, and they enjoyed a freedom most city kids would envy. After all, they lived at county fairs all summer long when most kids only got to see a fair once or twice a year.

Earlier this year, Grandpa had taken Samantha over to Santa Anita Park where she had applied for her exercise rider's license, so she could officially work her father's horses at the track. Unofficially, she had been exercising horses at the ranch since she was twelve.

Samantha had been especially excited about this year's trip because of Sierra Warrior, a two-year-old colt she had raised herself. In fact, she had practically saved his life. She remembered that day like it was yesterday.

After a very difficult birth in which the front tendons in the foal's legs were so contracted he couldn't stand, the vet and her dad had agreed that it would be merciful to put the poor baby horse to sleep. *Euthanize* was the word they used, a word she had vowed to hate forever. Fighting back huge tears, Samantha had begged them not to do it, for this was the best-bred, best-looking colt they'd ever had. And, at less than an hour old, he had already stolen her heart.

Unlike some solid-colored foals that had been born at the ranch, this one was a real Appaloosa from his striped hooves to the mottled skin on his belly. His coat was coal black with a white peacock-spotted blanket that covered his hindquarters, and his eyes had the white sclera that made his expression look almost human. They had to keep him; they just had to.

And so, Dr. Evans had put casts on both front legs, and Samantha had milked the mare and bottle-fed the baby until he was able to nurse by himself a month later. She called him "Chugalug" because he was such a greedy little rascal.

11

Every day, she made sure his barn stall was deep with fresh straw so he wouldn't injure himself in the struggle to get up and down for naps. She even put old zipper-front sweatshirts on him to keep him warm at night. That was a sight – a little spotted baby horse snuggled contentedly in the straw, wearing a sweatshirt that advertised, "Race An Appaloosa!" He repaid her kindness with an eager, heart-melting whinny whenever he saw her.

From being handled every day, the colt became so tame he would stand at the gate and beg to come into the backyard just to be with people. Samantha brushed and petted him and took him for long walks to exercise and strengthen his legs. She figured that over his first six months, she had put hundreds of miles on both of them, and both of them benefited. Chuggy, as she called him, grew stronger every day, and she buckled down to her schoolwork so she would have time to work with him.

As a future racehorse, the colt had much to learn in the first two years of his life before he went to the track. She became his enthusiastic teacher and best friend. Under her training, he learned not to nip or kick and to follow easily when led. After she had fed him in the horse trailer a few times, he jumped in eagerly at her command.

One of the most important lessons was to stand quietly and allow the horse shoer to work on his feet because, like human fingernails, horses hooves had to be trimmed regularly. Chug liked Doug, the farrier, well enough, but he didn't much care for what Doug had to do. He would lean his head on Samantha's shoulder, his eyes would glaze over, and he'd just get heaver and heaver as he relaxed all of his weight on her. With her arms around the colt in what she called a "Chug hug," she'd just brace her feet and scratch his neck while the farrier snipped away at the colt's overgrown feet.

"One of these days you're going to have to just dump him and let him fall," Doug had said with a laugh as the colt grew bigger and heavier, but it hadn't been necessary. Chug seemed to sense when he had gotten too heavy for her. Now, he just rested his chin lightly on her shoulder or stood quietly for shoeing when she wasn't there.

These days, the name Sierra Warrior suited the youngster better than Chuggy, however. He was big and beautiful, and unlike some of their other Appaloosas whose coats had changed, he had kept his black and white color. The black was inherited from his Thoroughbred dam, Sierra Princess, a mare they had bought from Cal Reed, an old friend of Grandpa's who owned Las Palmas Ranch a few miles down the road. The spots came from the Appaloosa stallion, War Eagle, who was standing at stud at another nearby ranch. Both of his parents were race winners, and Samantha just knew Chuggy was going to be the best, the very, very best.

As he turned two and began his track training, his timed workouts at the ranch had been excellent. Little by little, Samantha could tell her father was beginning to appreciate the confidence she had always had in her colt. After much persuasion, she had talked her parents into spending the money to nominate the colt into the California-Bred Appaloosa Futurity. The event was an annual stakes race for two-year-olds to be held in August at Bay Meadows Race Track during the San Mateo County Fair.

Her memories of happier times were suddenly interrupted by a scary thought. *What if Dad's not here to train him? What then?* The appearance of her mother's brother brought her abruptly back to the present.

"Hey, Sweetheart. How's my girl?" he called. Arms outstretched, he rushed up the walk, picked her up and swung her around. The big bear hug was not unwelcome.

"Uncle Jack," she protested weakly. "Put me down. I'm too big for this." Secretly, she enjoyed the attention, and she adored her jolly uncle.

She laughed in spite of her gloomy mood because, well, nobody could stay grouchy when big Jack Malone was around. His ready smile and the twinkle in his blue eyes could melt an iceberg. He set her back on her feet with a tickle to her ribs.

Samantha was not to be joshed out of finding out what was going on, however. She tilted her head back to look up at him and asked, "Where's my dad?"

Chapter II

A TRAINER IN TROUBLE

66Sweetheart, I flat don': have a clue," Jack Malone admitted, with a puzzled look and a shake of his head. He unlocked the door and motioned her inside. Samantha stepped quickly into their home away from home, her mind racing with a gazillion unanswered questions.

"So what's all this trouble everyone's talking about?" she demanded, sitting down at the dinette. "And where's Dad? Is Chug all right?"

"Hang on a minute," her uncle replied. He opened the fridge and took out a couple of Cokes. He handed one to Samantha as he squeezed his big frame into the booth opposite her. Taking off his straw Stetson, he ran his fingers through his black curly hair. Then he took a long drink of his soda while his niece just fidgeted with hers. The suspense was driving her nuts.

"Come on, Uncle Jack. Let's have it."

"Well, to put it bluntly," the big man said awkwardly. "Somebody dosed Pinky Mason's colt Saturday, and the horse almost died. They found a plastic jug with your dad's fingerprints all over it in the trashcan at the end of the barn. To make matters worse, they also found his keys buried in the straw when they raked the stall."

"Oh man." Samantha was shocked. She felt like crying, not because she believed the story, but because she was heartbroken to think anyone else would. *Poor Dad. He must feel awful.* Frank Kelly was one of the most respected trainers on the fair circuit. He was quick to lend a hand when anyone needed it, and his record had always been spotless.

Tears, however, were not generally an option for Samantha Kelly. She was a problem solver, not a whiner. "It's a setup," she scoffed in disgust.

"Course it's a setup," her uncle agreed. "For one thing, those keys have been missing since we ran in Stockton last month. Your dad had a new set made off mine. But some folks are believing it. You know they're always jealous 'cause your dad's a winner."

"My dad's a winner because he's a good trainer, and he works hard at it," Samantha argued. "Besides why would anyone drug one of Pinky's horses anyway? He's never had a good one since he quit riding."

"Oh, he's got a good one this year," her uncle stated emphatically. "Outworked Chug last week."

"No kidding?" Samantha was surprised and a little disappointed to hear that bit of news. "Is Pinky's colt going to be all right?"

"Yeah, he's gonna make it," her uncle answered, "but he probably won't be back in time for the Cal-Bred."

"So what did the stewards do to my dad?" the girl asked. Nervously, she bent the pop-top of the soda can back and forth until it snapped off with a metallic click. She dropped it into a cup on the table where they saved rings for Ronald McDonald House.

"They suspended his license," Uncle Jack replied. "The hearing's set for two weeks from now. Looks like we're out of the Cal-Bred too."

No way! Not Dad! She knew that losing his license was just about the worst thing that could happen to a trainer.

"It's too pat, too perfect," the girl said sharply. She slid out of the dinette and walked over to the sink. Things like this didn't happen to the Kellys; they happened to other people. She needed to think. She ran some water and squirted some soap on the breakfast dishes Uncle Jack had left. "Anyone who knows my dad knows he'd never hurt a horse," she said over her shoulder.

"People can be mean, Sweetheart," Uncle Jack said. "They like to see the big ones brought down, and they always back the underdog."

Well, Pinky Mason surely is an underdog.

Samantha thought Pinky was a likeable enough young man. He had quit being a jockey three years ago because he couldn't maintain a low weight. Then he started training, but he wasn't very good at it. Trouble was, like many jockeys, Pinky thought every horse that could run a little was star material. He came back every year, just knowing he had at least one world-beater in his stable. It hadn't been likely most of the time, since his horses were usually second-stringers. They belonged to one of the owners he had ridden a lot of years for who just wanted to help Pinky get started as a trainer.

The racetrack was like that, though, always taking care of its own. It was like a big family where there was always a place for someone down on his luck. The job might be grooming horses or acting as a valet in the jockeys' room, but no race tracker ever had to go hungry. Samantha had always felt like she was part of that big family, but judging from Mrs. Wilson's reaction to seeing her this afternoon, she wondered if all that was changing now.

Of course, Mrs. Wilson was a little bit of a snob. Her husband trained *only* Thoroughbreds, no Quarter Horses or Appaloosas. Before Tracy was born, her mother had ridden hunter-jumpers on the show circuit. She'd been talented enough to try out for the U.S. Equestrian Team but had given it all up to get married. Samantha's mother always said Barbara Wilson was probably disappointed and bitter that she hadn't followed her dream.

With the dishes done, Samantha turned back to her uncle. "So why did my dad disappear anyway?"

"Well, Sweetheart, it's been just plain awful. No one would talk to him. They gave him dirty looks and made remarks behind his back. No one would ride for him either. When we went into the kitchen in the morning, everyone just ignored us or moved to other tables. I guess he just couldn't take it anymore. I know I've made myself pretty scarce since Saturday."

"I know how you feel," Samantha admitted. "Tracy's mom ran me off a little while ago." *This is so bizarre. It's not like Dad to quit and run away.*

"Aw, Sweetheart," Uncle Jack sympathized, "I'm so sorry."

Her uncle crunched his empty soda can and dunked it neatly into the wastebasket near the door. "We were hoping you wouldn't be here during all of this. Frank said he was gonna call your mom and tell you not to come until Santa Rosa," he said. "That's why I didn't come to the bus station."

"Maybe he tried," his niece replied. "We weren't home. We spent the night at Aunt Becky's in Riverside. Anyhow, I'm glad I came. Somebody's got to work Chug."

"Aw, Sam, what's the point? He can't run without a trainer."

"We'll get Nick Wright to train him," she argued.

"Can't," her uncle said. "He didn't show up this year. Some kind of woman trouble."

"Well, then, we'll just have to train him ourselves," she insisted.

"I'm sorry," Uncle Jack said, a little embarrassed. "I just never did pass the trainer test. I tried I three times, but I freeze up every time I try to take the written part. Me and tests just don't get along."

"I'll help you pass the test," Samantha said confidently. "It's the only way." Uncle Jack just shook his head sadly and looked down at his hands.

"Uncle Jack," she pleaded, "we've got to run in that futurity. We've had Chug nominated in the Cal-Bred since he was just a baby. We can't give up now."

This year's futurity purse was worth close to $50,000. The winner's share would help her college fund substantially. Samantha wanted to become a vet, and that would take at least eight years of schooling and a lot of money. She planned to get her trainer's license as soon as she was old enough and work summers for her father to help out with the finances.

But it wasn't just the money. Samantha was certain that Chug was the best horse they'd ever owned. He deserved a chance to show what he could do. She glanced wistfully at his picture hanging next to the window. Her mother had framed it next to a poem Samantha had written when the colt was a long yearling.

The Yearlings
In the spring of the year, the babies come,
When the grass is fresh and green,
And to watch them frolic on wobbly legs,
Is the merriest sight I have seen.

In summer they grow, for the days are long,
And there's warmth and strength in the sun,
And in spite of the way their mamas fret,
They spend most of their days on the run.

The very first winter is spooky and strange,
For their world has turned crispy and white,
But its fun to make tracks and see smoke when they blow,
Then snuggle with mama at night.

In the spring of the year, new babies arrive,
But our yearlings are sturdy and strong.
With a toss of their heads, they gallop away,
To follow the restless wind's song.

Samantha heard Uncle Jack cough, and then he looked at his watch. "Last race's over. I think I'll go over to The Paddock and see if I can find a friendly face."

Samantha remembered that The Paddock was a bar across from the fairgrounds where horsemen hung out after the races. She also remembered that, in spite of his general good nature, Jack Malone could get his Irish up when he'd had a few. And with things the way they were, he might justify easing his troubles with a drink or two. "Well, don't get into any fights."

"You're shaming me girl," he said as he put on his hat. "I give up drinking last year."

She wanted to say, "again," but held her tongue. Her uncle had fallen off the wagon a time or two before. As he stepped out of the door, she called after him. "Where's Chug?"

"Barn C," came the answer as the screen door banged shut.

Samantha snatched the spare house key off a hook just inside the door, stuffed it in her pocket and headed for the stables, anxious to find her horse. Seeing Chug would help take her mind off their trouble, at least for a little while. She smiled as she thought about him.

Appaloosas! I love 'em! I don't care what anybody says. Apps are just the best!

Samantha recalled her dad telling her when she was just a little girl that Appaloosas were one of the oldest breeds in the world. He said ancient cave drawings in France from as far back as 20,000 years pictured horses with spots on them. They were also featured in ancient Chinese art.

When the Spanish introduced horses to this continent, the animals eventually became an integral part of American Indian life. The Nez Perce and Palouse tribes of the Pacific Northwest had been especially fond of spotted horses, and it was said that they were the first tribes to selectively breed for intelligence, speed and endurance, all qualities prized in the modern Appaloosa.

White settlers arriving in the land of the Nez Perce and Palouse people would see spotted horses near the Palouse River or horses owned by the Palouse Tribe, and they started saying "a Palouse horse" or "a Palousey horse." Over the years, the name became "Appaloosey" and then "Appaloosa."

Spotted horses were among those that carried the Nez Perce over the Chief Joseph Trail during the Nez Perce War of 1877, when the Indians eluded the U.S. Calvary over some 1300 miles of rugged terrain, trying to reach Canada and freedom. Samantha always thought it was a really sad story and found herself siding with the Indians when she watched the movie "I Will Fight No More Forever," detailing their amazing trip.

Lovers of the spotted horse founded The Appaloosa Horse Club in 1938. Grandpa's old friend, Cal Reed, had given Samantha quite a bit of information on the early days of the club because he had known Claude Thompson, one of the founders. She had written a term paper on her favorite breed last year that had earned her an "A." And the writing had been easy because she was so crazy about the horses, she could go on about them for hours.

Back in January, Samantha had spent weeks researching and making an authentic Nez Perce Indian outfit to wear in the annual Horseweek Parade in April. She rode one of her mother's spotted mares in the parade and won first place in her class. Now, she was considered the school expert on the breed, but she always told people that Cal Reed had forgotten more about the Appaloosa horse than she'd ever know.

And Chug's the prettiest one I've ever seen. She smiled with pride as she hurried along toward the barns.

Chapter III

A GORGEOUS COLT!

Walking along the shed rows, Samantha was thinking she loved the peaceful backstretch now, late in the day, almost as much as in the busy morning. The last race was over, and the horses had been fed, leaving the barn area pretty much deserted. Most of the trainers and their help were either over at The Paddock, out to dinner with an owner or having supper at home in their RVs.

Samantha reflected on how exciting returning to the track each summer had always been in the past. She looked forward to it like city kids looked forward to going to a summer camp in the mountains. She loved getting up at the crack of dawn and going out to feed the horses in the crispy morning air.

As the backstretch awoke for the day, she would smell bacon cooking in the track restaurant everyone called "the kitchen" and hear pots and pans banging around inside. Hay delivery trucks, water trucks wetting down the dust and men shouting as they loaded or unloaded horses all added to the busy, noisy atmosphere of the barn area early in the day.

She enjoyed watching exercise riders on frisky Thoroughbreds and Quarter Horses and Appaloosas greet each other with a wave or a nod as they made their way out to the track for morning workouts. And she laughed at the horses that were left behind in the barns because they stomped and neighed impatiently as the grooms hauled hay and grain from stall to stall.

She and her father would each have a steaming cup of cocoa to tide them over until the morning work was done. Then he and Uncle Jack would head for the track kitchen to look over *The Daily Racing Form,* a tabloid size newspaper that was practically the racing Bible. Over breakfast, the men would discuss upcoming race conditions with the other trainers. Samantha would head out to find Tracy or go over to Ida Mae's to see what new craft project she had in the works.

She glanced up as she passed Ida Mae's trailer on her way to see Chug and thought about going in, but it looked dark. *Too bad. I bet Ida Mae wouldn't snub me.*

Her friend, Ida Mae Tyler, was from Texas, with a southern drawl that just wouldn't quit. She said, "y'all" even when there was only one person present and called everybody younger than her, "darling," only it came out sounding something like, "dawlin." When Ann Kelly had stopped coming to the track, Ida Mae had sort of adopted Samantha. The other track kids were always welcome too, but Samantha was her favorite.

Ann Kelly always said that while the sun hadn't been especially good to Ida Mae, who had been a horsewoman all her life, her kindness and generosity made people forget the wrinkles in her deeply tanned face. She had a warm smile and blue eyes that sparkled when she ran into someone she liked, which was most people.

Ida Mae had been a champion barrel racer when she was younger and had been absolutely certain at that time that the American Quarter Horse was the best working horse in the country. When she had married race trainer Tommy Tyler many years ago, she had decided that Quarter Horses were the best runners as well. Oh, they trained a few Appaloosas, but those Apps usually had Quarter Horse breeding and ran shorter distances. On many occasions, Samantha had heard her dad and the Tylers arguing in a friendly way about the relative good qualities of each breed.

The Tylers didn't have any children of their own, but Ida Mae always had fresh cookies and a lot of love for the children at the racetrack. Her trailer was neat as a pin, and it always smelled good, like something really yummy was in the oven just waiting for a hungry youngster to taste.

Around horses, Ida Mae was as tough as any man, but Samantha knew that at home, she was decidedly feminine. Her little trailer was decorated with lacy curtains, country-style pictures and beautiful afghans she had crocheted.

One summer, when it had rained solid for several weeks and everyone was stuck indoors, Ida Mae had taught her young friend how to crochet. Samantha smiled as she remembered how surprised her mother had been when she returned home that fall and presented Ann Kelly with a pretty granny square afghan she had made herself. She hadn't told her mother about how many times she had pulled out whole rows and done them over, however.

Thinking about Ida Mae gave Samantha an idea. *Maybe Tommy would train Chug for them.*

Her pace picked up as she rounded the corner of the third row of barns. Just for an instant, she thought she saw the old cowboy with the gray beard and cane hobbling along down at the other end of the shed row. He disappeared so quickly, however, she decided she had been imagining things. *Quit being so spooky, Samantha Kelly.*

As always, a surge of pride filled Samantha as her eyes settled on the green and white guards that kept the horses confined in the Kelly barns. They were stretched across the doorways, advertising for all to see that inside each stall there was a Kelly horse from Limerick Farms. In the middle of the heavy rubber guards there were big green shamrocks, each with a white capital "L" in the center. This was her family's logo and reminded them all of where the first of their branch of the Kelly family had lived in Ireland. Grandpa used the same logo on his dairy farm, which was just down the road from the younger Kellys' ranch down south in Riverside County.

She smiled as her eyes searched the shed row for Chug, but none of the horses was looking out of the stall doors. A steady "crunch, crunch," told her that they were all enjoying their supper.

Well, at least we've still got a groom to feed the horses. I'll have to look up Joey as soon as I see Chug.

She peeked into the first stall and saw a big, black and white leopard Appaloosa. His head was stuck deep into hay net at the back of the stall.

"Hey, boy, come here," she coaxed, but the big horse just kicked a hind leg out in her general direction and never missed a bite. "See how you are," she kidded with a laugh.

She figured the horse must be Harlequin D owned by Dr. Davidson. Her dad had told her the big gelding was a good, solid runner who always brought home a paycheck.

Actually, most of the horses her father trained did belong to other people. When her grandfather was training Thoroughbreds, he never owned a single horse except the pony horse he rode to accompany horses he was training to the track. Truth be known, Frank Kelly probably would have liked it that way too, but Samantha's mother was a softy when it came to babies. She kept her mares bred, carefully researching pedigrees and always trying to find the very best bloodlines. As a result, they usually had a colt or two of their own at the racetrack.

The Kellys had started with a couple of Appaloosa broodmares Ann owned when they got married. Samantha had learned to ride on those gentle mares, riding behind her mother as soon as she was big enough to hang on. Before marrying Ann, Frank had generally trained Thoroughbreds. When his wife wanted to breed for Appaloosa runners, he was willing to go along with her. But he knew they'd have to have more racing blood to enhance their speed.

They had looked for the best Thoroughbred stallions to breed to, but it had been tough. Most Thoroughbred stallion owners would not offer stud service to any other breed except maybe a really fast, winning Quarter Horse mare.

Grandpa had told Samantha that Cal Reed had made things a lot easier for California's Appaloosa breeders in the beginning. Cal trained both breeds at Las Palmas. He conditioned and trained the racehorses, and his son, Will, handled the show string and gave lessons. Cal always said the Thoroughbreds paid the bills, but that he just flat liked the Appaloosas. He liked their color, and he liked their disposition, and he liked their spunk. His personal mount was always an Appaloosa horse.

When the Appaloosa Horse Club had decided to allow solid-colored horses of Appaloosa breeding to be blood-typed to confirm their pedigrees and then shown and raced, Cal had been outraged. He contended that their color was one of the things that made them special. He and Frank Kelly had argued for hours about it because previously, the Kellys had either given away foals that had been born solid-colored or kept them for breeding only. Samantha's father had argued that he was tired of throwing away well-bred babies whose only fault was that they weren't spotted.

Most of the time, it was the outcrossing to other breeds that caused the problem, but both horsemen agreed they needed the infusion of good racing blood to get good racing Appaloosas. Actually, even though Cal was the one who had made it easier to find Thoroughbred stallions, he was still willing to keep the solids and breed them back to Appaloosas, hoping for color in the next generation.

Cal had gotten a foot in the door with Thoroughbred stallion owners when he'd offered Appaloosa nurse mares to suckle extremely valuable Thoroughbred babies whose dams had either died or couldn't provide enough nourishment for their foals. The Thoroughbred owners had been so grateful that when Cal had asked to breed his Appaloosa mares to their stallions, they had agreed, if somewhat reluctantly. The little mare Samantha found in the next barn stall was the result of just such a breeding.

She was a pretty bay mare with a big white blanket over her hindquarters, and she was one of Samantha's favorites. When the girl called her, the mare turned and came over to the stall door, a wisp of alfalfa still sticking out of the corner of her mouth.

"Hi, Baby," Samantha cooed, reaching up and scratching the mare behind both ears. In turn, the horse nuzzled the girl's neck. Samantha figured she now had a green collar, but hey, collars were washable, weren't they?

"How are you, Sweetheart?" she cooed, but as she spoke, another horse a few doors down started making a fuss.

"Chuggy!" Samantha squealed, jogging over to his stall. "How's my big boy?" The colt was practically dancing in his eagerness to be near her. His eyes were bright, and his ears twitched forward at the sound of her voice. She unhooked the stall guard and quickly slipped inside his stall, fastening the latch behind her.

"Have you missed me, boy?" she murmured, wrapping her arms around his neck and burying her face in his silky coat. Chug nuzzled her hair, making little rumbly sounds in his throat, and Samantha was so thrilled to be with her horse again, she almost forgot the bad day she'd been having. Then, just as suddenly, he turned and went back to his hay.

"You big piggy!" she scolded playfully. "You haven't seen me in three months and all you can think about is food!" The colt turned and bobbed his head up and down as if to agree.

"Still a clown," she laughed. Chug just turned back to his supper, which gave the girl a chance to examine him more carefully.

He's grown, and he looks so fit. His black coat is as shiny as a new piano key, and his white spots look freshly painted. Is he taller? Maybe, and just look at those leg muscles.

It was getting harder and harder to remember the tiny, pitiful little thing that had teetered around on his bandaged legs begging for a bottle. But she'd never forget warm summer days when he was a yearling, and she had walked him for miles, enjoying the fresh air and listening to the sounds of the outdoors. As the colt got stronger, so did Samantha. After leading him around and holding him when he spooked, the girl had arm muscles that wouldn't quit. The exercise had helped her softball game, and being strong had other advantages too. Her father had let her saddle-break the horse.

It hadn't been all that difficult, really. She had been rubbing him down with big towels and throwing them over his face since he was a baby so he wouldn't be afraid of things like saddle blankets and pads. She'd leaned her weight gently on him until he was used to the feel of something on his back. She'd even walked him out with a bareback pad on, so he wouldn't mind a cinch when it was time to learn to accept a saddle as well. So saddling the colt hadn't been a problem, but the bit, well, that was another matter. Her dad had finally stepped in when she couldn't get Chug to let her bridle him.

With a lifetime's experience handling horses, Frank had rubbed a little molasses on the bit and deftly slipped it into the colt's mouth. Chug had tongued the sweet syrup, with what Samantha was sure was a grin on his face, not minding the bit at all. Frank then tied the reins to the Western saddle they used for training. At first, Chug had tried to resist the restraint, but when he found his struggles useless, he had just started circling the round pen with first Frank, and then Samantha, handling the long lines.

Frank said, "Well, he's not just pretty; he's smart too."

Chug was the first horse Samantha had ever tried to saddle-break, correction – saddle train. Her father had told her many times that you don't break a horse.

She hadn't been sure what Chug would do when she mounted him for the first time. As she put her foot in the stirrup, visions of rodeo bucking horses filled her mind. She swung her leg over and gingerly wiggled down into the saddle while her dad held the bridle. Frank had led the horse forward a few steps.

"Okay, let him go," she said, holding her breath in anticipation of a wild ride.

The wild ride never happened. In fact, the colt just kind of tippy-toed around the arena trying to keep his balance with the unaccustomed weight on his back. She gave the reins a little slack and squeezed with her legs to encourage him into a steady walk. He thought that was okay, but when she clucked to him and squeezed harder, he stepped sideways a few quick steps. A less-experienced rider might have been unseated, but Samantha stuck to the saddle like glue.

With patient urging, she had gotten the colt into a slow trot. "Woo-hoo!" she shouted as she passed her father who had stayed in the round pen just in case she needed him. After that, the rest had been easy, and Frank had allowed her to be the colt's exercise rider, even though he had an ex-jockey who came every morning to work the other horses.

Hard work and patience do pay off. Chug was fast and strong, yet easy to handle. She was sure he was going to be a winner.

"You are so gorgeous," she said out loud. "What a picture we're going to have when you win the Cal-Bred."

"If you win," came a voice behind her. She recognized the voice instantly.

Well, this tops off an all-around, really crummy day. She turned to face the intruder.

Chapter IV

MEET THE ENEMY

"Slade Lang," she said with a forced smile. "Who let you out of your cage?"

Unfazed, the tall boy answered with a sly grin, "Always the kidder, aren't you, Sammy?" He knew she hated to be called by that name. "How's it going?"

How's it going? He knows how it's going all right. Ooh, if I could just tell him how I really feel about seeing him again, but Mom still says we have to be nice to the Lang boys because they don't have a mother.

Slade Lang had been her archenemy at the racetrack ever since the first time she had met him when she was just a little girl. She could remember that meeting like it was yesterday.

She and her mother had gotten dressed up for church that Sunday morning. It had been raining all night, and the backside was a quagmire. She was tippy-toeing out to the truck in her best shoes when along came this little kid on a dirt bike. He deliberately hit a puddle next to her just so he could give her a nice big, muddy splash.

"You stupid creep!" the little girl had shouted. She picked up a rock and was about to pelt him with it when her mother stopped her. Slade had just grinned and sped noisily away while her mother explained, "Samantha, we have to be nice to the Lang boys. They lost their mother a few months ago, you know."

From that day on, Slade Lang had teased her, tripped her and tortured her every chance he got. He flattened the tires on her new bike, drew mustaches with ink on the Barbies she had forgotten to bring inside, and wrote her nasty notes. Once, he had even thrown her tiny calico kitten out in front of the Monday morning trash truck because she had called him a redheaded freak.

Luckily, the driver had seen the little cat just in time and managed to screech the big truck to a noisy halt just as the kitten scurried across the street. He had given Slade a tongue lashing, but the boy just laughed, and sped away. His nasty pranks continued

– that is, until the summer Samantha was ten and Slade was eleven.

One Saturday morning, Slade had found a dead rabbit somewhere, probably down by the creek that bordered the track. It was half-eaten by coyotes and really gross, with grisly flesh and bones sticking out between tufts of scabby gray hair. He had tied a dirty piece of rope around what was left of its neck and surprised Samantha with it while she was mucking out a stall. "Here's a new pet for you, Sammy."

The girl had dropped her rake and run screaming toward the kitchen where her father and uncle were having breakfast. Slade followed, trying to touch her with the disgusting carcass as she fled. He had almost caught her, but just as they reached at the kitchen, Slade's father had come out. When he saw what was going on, he grabbed his son by the collar and jerked him clean up off the ground. Slade wailed for mercy, the dead rabbit still dangling from his right hand.

"Drop it!" his father commanded as he eased his son back down onto his feet.

Samantha could see that Slade was absolutely terrified. A powerful man, Jake Lang had then pulled his son close and threatened, "If I ever see you bothering that little girl again, I'm going to take a riding crop to your backside. You hear me, boy?" He tightened his grip on the boy's collar.

Slade squirmed and "ouched" and gave an affirmative shake of his head. "Now, say you're sorry to the little lady."

Slade's face was bright red, and his eyes were smarting with tears he was trying hard not to shed. "I'm sorry," he mumbled.

"Louder!"

"I'm sorry," the boy shouted at Samantha.

Her eyes grew big with surprise and shock. She just stood there, unable to utter a word because she had never seen a father act so cruelly toward his child. She'd never even been spanked in her entire life, and she couldn't imagine what it must be like to be so afraid of your own father.

Frank Kelly had come out of the kitchen just in time to hustle Samantha home before she burst into tears. And, from that day on, Slade confined his nasty ways to snide remarks when no one was nearby, and he always looked at her like he was planning something unpleasant.

Oddly enough, his younger brother, Jeff, had become one of Samantha's best friends. They had a lot in common; Slade picked on Jeff all the time, too. Neither one of them ever ratted Slade out, however, both fearing Jake Lang's quick temper.

Slade's next comment brought Samantha back to the present. "So, that's the hot colt your father's so jazzed about," he sneered. "Well, you high and mighty Kellys ain't going to be the big shots this year. My dad's got a horse that can flat run a hole in the wind. He already won two races, and he wasn't even winded when Jorge brought him back to the winner's circle."

Scratching Chug under his mane, Samantha studied the boy out of the corner of her eye as he boasted. His red, curly hair was still a mess, and the bane of teenagers everywhere, acne, had taken its toll on his freckled complexion. His once-white T-shirt was sweat-stained under the armpits, and bony knees poked out of his torn jeans. Even his hightops were worn and dirty, the laces half-tied. Over the winter, the boy had stretched out, but to Samantha's eyes, he hadn't improved much.

She was wondering about his brother, Jeff, when she heard another, somewhat familiar voice.

"You bothering Samantha?" Jeff inquired casually, walking up behind Slade.

The girl noticed that Jeff, too, had stretched out over the winter, and he was as tall as his brother. His squeaky, little-boy voice had become deeper, and in contrast to Slade, Jeff looked clean and neat. His reddish blond hair was combed, his shirt faded but ironed, and his jeans, while also faded, had no holes. And there was something else Samantha couldn't quite put her finger on – he looked, well, somehow more grown up.

"Hi Samantha," he said in a friendly, but strangely shy, manner.

"Hey, Jeff," she answered, feeling a little more comfortable now that the sunlight was beginning to fade. The idea of being alone with Slade Lang in a dark, deserted shed row gave her major goose bumps. She still did not and never would trust his brother, but Jeff was a friend.

"Good to see you, Jeff." Samantha turned her back on Slade in a deliberate attempt to exclude him from the conversation.

He mumbled, "I'm outta here. I'll just leave you two lovebirds alone," and shuffled off down the shed row, kicking at anything that got in his way.

"So that's Sierra Warrior?" Jeff said, trying to hide the embarrassment caused by his brother's remark. Her father always said Jeff had been in love with Samantha Kelly since the day he had met her. Frank kidded her about it, but she had assured him that Jeff was only a pal.

She had felt that way until just now. Suddenly, she found herself thinking that Jeff was really quite attractive, and by the way he was looking at her, she had a feeling the attraction might just be mutual. Then, remembering her ex-boyfriend, the girl quickly closed her mind to all thoughts of romance. She had too much to do to think about boys right now. She had to find her father, get his name cleared, and help get Chug ready for the big race.

"Isn't he gorgeous?" she asked nervously. Jeff was staring at her, and it was making her a little uncomfortable. She caught the colt's head and posed him sideways. "We call him Chugalug because he's got such an appetite."

"He *is* nice," Jeff agreed, looking quickly from the girl to the horse.

"Slade said your dad has a good colt this year too." She loosed Chug, and the horse went back to cleaning up his supper.

"Yep," Jeff answered. "He sire is War Eagle just like Chug's. Name's Warhawk, and he can run a little". To say a horse can run a little was the horsemen's way of avoiding bad luck by bragging. "Broke his maiden first time out."

"Wow!" Samantha exclaimed, knowing that horses rarely won their first races. She found herself wishing that Chug had been raced, but her dad had only worked the colt, waiting for the right race. He was looking for just the right conditions – not too far, not too much weight, and a nice, firm track. "When can I see Warhawk?"

"Come out to the track tomorrow," Jeff answered. "He'll be galloping in the morning."

"Cool!" Samantha was anxious to see Chug's half-brother.

Jeff looked carefully at the Kelly colt again. "You know, Sam, they're practically twins."

"Really?" said Samantha. "Who's his dam?"

"He's out of mom's old mare, Sierra Moon Runner," he answered. From the name, Samantha knew that the mare had to be Las Palmas stock and was probably related to her mother's mares. Then Jeff added, a little sadly, "He was her last foal. She died last winter."

In the light from the corner of the barn, Samantha could see Jeff's brown eyes growing a little misty. "Dad's put every dime he's got into this horse," the boy continued. "So far, he's paying his way, but we sure need to do well in the Cal-Bred to keep things going."

Samantha wanted to change the subject because she was beginning to have some very mixed feelings about the race. Not winning the Cal-Bred might mean putting college off for a year for her, but somehow she knew, not winning the Cal-Bred might break the Langs for good.

Although some of the race trackers thought the Langs were a bunch of losers, her father had told her that Jake Lang knew his horses and was a good trainer. Trouble was that ever since his wife died, he'd been filled with bitterness and just didn't seem to care anymore. It had been over ten years, and you would think he would have gotten over her death somewhat, but he never did. As a result, he just couldn't get along with anybody and lost owners right and left. The boys had practically raised themselves, and people felt sorry for them. Jeff had told her that all their pity really irked his brother, but Samantha didn't want to dwell on Slade right now.

It was a beautiful, warm night, and she wouldn't be able to find out anything about her father until the California Horse Racing Board office opened in the morning anyway. She needed to do something to kill time and get her mind off the day's events.

"You want to go over to the carnival and toss some baseballs?" she asked. "I might even let you beat me."

Jeff laughed. Samantha was always tough competition. From working with horses all her life, she had a right arm that was probably as strong as his, and she could toss a ball at a carnival milk bottle with the accuracy of a major league all-star.

"I'd ask Tracy, but her mom won't let her talk to me," Samantha added.

"She can talk to me," said Jeff with a grin. "Meet us at the gate in ten minutes."

* * *

A short time later, the three old friends were walking arm in arm down the midway, reminiscing about all the good times they had shared over the years. The rides were in full swing, and the midway was bright, noisy and exciting. They could hear the clicks and whirrs of the rides, music from the carousel, and hawkers touting their wares. "Getch ya corn dogs here!" shouted a red-faced man in front of a hot dog stand. It was fun to be back.

"Remember when we stood in line twelve times for free ice cream in Santa Rosa?" Tracy said with a giggle, her dimples popping up on either side of what Samantha had always regarded, a little enviously, as a really cute smile. "I had barely stuffed the end of the 11th mini-cone in my mouth when you pushed me in front of you, Sam. I had to say 'thank you' out of the corner of my mouth, and you couldn't stop laughing."

"Remember when you took a big bite out of the overstuffed hamburger and it slipped out of the bun and ketchuped your white blouse, Sam?" Jeff reminded her.

"What about you," she retorted, "when you were in the watermelon eating contest and then barfed all the way home?"

Talking about old times took their minds off more serious matters for a little while as they strolled around the carnival midway, looking over the many things for sale and stopping at the food stands.

Neither Samantha nor Jeff won anything at the milk can throw, but they had a good time trying.

Later, when they were on their way home, Tracy stopped them. "I just want you to know that I don't believe all that junk they're saying about your dad, Sam."

Samantha looked at her friend gratefully. Tracy, whose big brown eyes were usually merry, and lately, outrageously flirty, was wearing a serious expression. Jeff, handsome, grown up Jeff, was suddenly quiet too.

"Me neither," he added, "and I'll deck Slade if says any more about it."

Samantha was visibly moved by their oaths of loyalty and just stood there, not knowing what to say. In fact, all three of them seemed at an embarrassing loss for words until Tracy piped up, "Group hug!"

And Jeff said, "To the Three Musketeers; all for one and one for all."

They hugged and laughed, and then Tracy started to sing, "Who's the leader of the club that's made for you and me…"

"M-i-c-k-e-y, M-o-u-s-e," they sang in unison as they walked along, arm in arm, toward home. Tracy was laughing so hard, she could hardly sing, and Samantha, helpless with the giggles, spilled what was left of her popcorn. It was the most fun she'd had since she arrived at the fair.

And then she saw him again, the old cowboy with the gray beard and the cane. He was standing under the light at the end of the lane.

"Trace," she said in a whisper, grabbing her friend's arm so hard that Tracy winced. "Do you know who that old guy over there is?"

But when her friend turned to look, the man was nowhere in sight. "What guy?" asked Tracy.

"Oh, never mind." Samantha tried to act casual. "I guess I'm just imagining things. See you tomorrow." She walked toward her father's coach, still wondering who the old guy was and why he seemed to be following her.

Chapter V

PLEASE GOD, I NEED SOME HELP HERE

Samantha was glad to see the lights were still on when she walked in the door about eleven o'clock. The mysterious old cowboy had given her a bad case of the creeps. Uncle Jack was sitting at the table playing solitaire on the laptop. She remembered how cozy the coach was when her dad was there, and she would listen while he and Uncle Jack discussed the upcoming races. *I miss him so much.*

"Hey, Sam," Uncle Jack greeted the girl. "Glad you're home. I was beginning to get a little worried."

"Jeff and Tracy and I went over to the midway," she said, closing the door. "Uncle Jack, have you seen an old cowboy with a gray beard hanging around the backstretch? He limps and has to use a cane."

"Can't say as I have," came the reply. "Why do you ask?"

"I don't know," she answered. "I just seem to be seeing him everywhere, like he's following me or something."

Uncle Jack looked up and gave his niece a reassuring smile. Then, his expression became momentarily thoughtful. "Probably just some old race tracker looking for someone he knows. You know how those old guys just can't stay away from the track. I wouldn't worry about it."

She said, "You're probably right," and started for the loft. She'd seen those has-beens and "wanna-bes" every summer - ex-trainers, worn-out jockeys, people who could never completely give up the exhilaration of racing horses. Who could blame them? Horse racing was the most exciting thing in her life too.

"Wait, Sam," her uncle called after her. "I-uh-well, did Annie send any money up with you? I'm kinda broke."

"Oh, I'm sorry, Uncle Jack. I've got your paycheck in my suitcase. I'll get it."

Samantha's mother, Ann Kelly, was the bookkeeper in the family. While Frank was an excellent trainer, she always said he messed up the checkbook every time he used it. She said she shuddered to think what might happen if he had an ATM card. To keep everything straight, she had taken over the family finances as soon as they were married.

Frank would send her most of the purse money he won, and his owners would send their training money directly to the ranch. Then Ann would send Frank, Jack and Joey's paychecks up to them at whatever fair they were currently working. With her careful handling of the money, the Kellys were always able to pay their bills on time in spite of the sometimes-erratic way the money might come in.

Occasionally, Frank would admit that his gentle Annie was a little tight when it came to money, especially when the other trainers kidded him about being "kept on a short leash." However, when he looked at some of his friends who couldn't handle money and were always behind in their bills, he figured Annie was doing the right thing. And, he could almost always talk her out of a little extra money for a real emergency, like claiming a really good horse he'd had his eye on.

Samantha's Uncle Jack had never had his sister's calm head for business either. "Easy come, easy go," was his motto, and he rarely had any extra cash. He liked to bet on the horses, which could be a deadly game if you were at the track every day. Sometimes he won, but more often than not, he lost. He had also lost two wives due to his drinking and gambling. Now that he had joined Alcoholics Anonymous, he had a little more spending money, but he either loaned it to friends or bought presents for his family.

Samantha would never forget the day he quit drinking for good. He said it had really been hard to stand up in a room full of strangers and say, "I'm Jack Malone, and I'm an alcoholic." She always thought that would be even harder than standing alone in front of Miss Saylor's English class reading one of her poems. When she had to speak in public, Samantha always got weak-kneed and light-headed. It made her dizzy just thinking about it.

To stay busy and keep sober over the winter, Uncle Jack had quit his winter bartending job in Reno and gone to work at the Kelly ranch. He had completed a lot of projects at the ranch too. The white rail fence that surrounded the pasture was mended and freshly painted, and the tractor they used to grade the training track was in tip-top mechanical shape.

He'd even helped put in a foaling stall at the far end of the barn, complete with closed circuit television. Now, from the office or house, they could watch the mares that were due to foal. Uncle Jack had also stopped going out at night and now spent the evenings with the family, challenging all comers to a fast game of Trivial Pursuit. He almost always won, and Samantha suspected he had memorized all the answers when no one was looking. She planned to get a new version before next winter.

Samantha found herself wondering if, now that he was back at the track around his old drinking buddies, he could stay off the booze, especially in light of all the trouble they were having. She could only hope.

When she returned to the kitchen and handed her uncle his check, he was all smiles. He took it out of the envelope, looked it over and folded it in half. Tucking it into the pocket of his Western shirt, he snapped the flap shut and picked up his hat.

"Thank you, Sam. I think I'll just go on over to The Paddock and get this cashed so I have some money for tomorrow."

He seemed in a hurry, and Samantha was just too tired to question him or start an argument about where he was going. She climbed up into the loft that was her bedroom and fished around in her suitcase for one of the oversize T-shirts she usually wore to bed. After changing clothes, she snuggled under the patchwork quilt Grandma had made for her from scraps she had saved from Samantha's little-girl dresses. Then, she closed her eyes, trying desperately to get some much-needed sleep.

Unfortunately, her brain had other ideas. Try as she might to make her mind a peaceful blank, she kept running over what had happened during the day. *Was it only this morning I left southern California?*

Added to what her uncle had already told her about her father's trouble, there were other things she had heard from Tracy and Jeff, awful things.

Jeff had told her he had been walking down at the end of Barn K the morning Pinky discovered his colt down in the stall.

"Oh my God!" He'd heard Pinky's astonished cry. He and several trainers had run to Pinky's aid.

"He's dying," Pinky wailed.

"I'll get the vet," said one of the trainers.

"Get the colt up right away!" another urged. "Keep him on his feet!" The three of them had pulled and tugged and smacked the young horse on the rump until he finally heaved to his feet and stood there trembling, his breathing rapid and erratic.

Jeff said the vet had treated the colt and told Pinky to keep him walking.

"It was so sad," Tracy added, "to see Pinky dragging that colt around all morning. When I saw him, he was actually crying. Can you imagine – a grown man crying right there in front of everybody?"

Samantha had cringed when she heard that. She couldn't begin to imagine a grown man crying, no matter what. All at once it hit her. What if something like that had happened to Chug? She would be inconsolable, and all her friends would be sympathetic. No wonder everyone was mad at her father. They were all imagining themselves in Pinky's shoes. Even though she understood, Samantha still felt bad when she thought about how Tracy's mother had treated her.

"And it's a shame," Jeff had continued. "He's a good colt. His works were as good as Warhawk's. I was really looking forward to seeing the three of them duke it out in the Cal-Bred. It would have been a great race."

Poor Pinky. He really was a nice guy, and everybody liked him. He always greeted Samantha with, "Hi Shorty," to which she would answer, "Taller than you." Then, they'd stand back to back to see who was taller. It was a game they had played since she was eight, and last year had been close. She was sure that this year she would be the tallest because by the end of school, most of her Levis were too short. Besides, Pinky wasn't going to grow anymore. He was old, pushing 25 at least.

*　　　*　　　*

Some time later during the night, Samantha was awakened by someone singing "Danny Boy" in a melodic, but very loud voice. *This has just got to be a bad dream.* The singing persisted. Then a neighbor shouted, "Go on home, Jack. It's after midnight."

Oh boy. Uncle Jack's off the wagon again!

Quickly, she grabbed her jacket and hurried toward the door. Stepping out into the chilly night, she could see her uncle weaving up the path to the house. Her bare feet hit a rock, and she mumbled something that would have shocked her mother.

"Nobody appreciates a good song anymore," Uncle Jack was saying as he teetered first to the right and then over-corrected to the left, almost losing his balance completely. Samantha put her arm around him and guided him through the doorway. The strong beer smell nearly gagged her.

Inside, she propped him up against a wall and hurried to make the couch into a bed.

"It's a sad thing, Sweetheart," the man continued, "when your friends won't let you sing anymore." He slid precariously to one side.

"Come on, Uncle Jack, lie down," she coaxed. When he had sunk down on the bed, she pulled off his hat and boots.

"And it's a sadder thing when a barkeep won't even let you have a little credit," he went on.

His speech was slurred, and from the red of his eyes and nose, Samantha knew he'd been drinking since he left her. "Go to sleep, Uncle Jack," she pleaded, but the man still wanted to talk.

"I cashed my paycheck, and those guys from Reno were right there waiting to take my money on account for what I owed them. Can you imagine that, Sam? Just take a guy's last dollar, they would, even after I done what they asked."

What's he talking about anyway? If he cashed his paycheck, he should have had several hundred dollars in his pocket.

A really scary thought entered her mind when she recalled Pinky's colt and what Uncle Jack had said about "doing what they'd asked." Quickly, she pushed the idea way, way back in her mind. Drunk or sober, there was no way her favorite uncle would ever hurt a horse. She tucked a blanket over him. He was already sound asleep, snoring lightly.

Turning off the light, she crept quietly up into her bed. Not a very faithful churchgoer, she knew that tonight she needed some help.

She prayed out loud. "Dear God, I know I don't go to church every Sunday, and I'm a terrible backslider like Mom says, but I've got a real mess here. Any little thing you could do to help me out would really be appreciated."

She closed her eyes and waited quietly, but no flash of insight was forthcoming. No lightning flashed, and her dad did not come walking tall and confidently through the door. All at once, Samantha felt very lonely and wished her mother or Grandpa was there. Either of them would set things right in a big hurry. She was certain of that. But she was being silly. Mom had to run the ranch and take James to Little League. And Grandpa? Um, Grandpa. She smiled. She would call her grandfather first thing in the morning, and right after that, she would go over to the California Horse Racing Board office and find out what the heck was going on.

Chapter VI

CHEER-UP, CHEERILY

Next morning, Samantha awoke early when a bright shaft of sunlight began to dance over her eyes. A little bird outside her window was singing, "Cheer-up, cheerily." It made her smile, and just for a moment she forgot about yesterday's troubles.

She pushed the curtains to one side of the little bedroom window and looked out at a beautiful day. It was California bright and sunny, with a blue and cloudless sky that flooded the room with light. She could see two gray squirrels chasing each other around and around on the pine tree next to their coach. When one squirrel ran up behind the other on a branch, it screeched and jumped straight up in the air. Samantha laughed out loud at their antics. Although the previous night had been chilly, when she opened the window, she discovered it was already quite warm outside.

After showering and putting on a tank top and a pair of jeans, she made her way into the kitchen past Uncle Jack, who was still sound asleep on the couch bed. She thought that was too bad because she really wanted to ask him about what he "had done" for those casino men. But it would just have to wait. She fixed herself a cup of instant cocoa and found a granola bar in the kitchen drawer. It was pretty stale.

She tried to call her grandfather, but no one answered. She didn't want to leave a message. His answer machine was kind of a hit and miss piece of equipment, and it usually frustrated Grandpa when he tried to use it. Besides, she didn't like the idea of leaving bad news on a machine. She headed out to the barns to find Joey, her father's new groom. She wanted to make sure he was keeping a careful watch on her father's horses. After what had been done to Pinky's horse, who knew what might happen next?

Joey Martin was the son of one of Frank Kelly's horse owners. Sadly, he had fried his once-bright mind with drugs and now had a very limited future. He'd been clean and sober for over a year, but he could only handle the simplest of jobs.

As a favor to his father, Frank had agreed to take Joey to the track and let him try his hand at being a groom. The only stipulation was that if he backslid even once, he would be packed off immediately. So far, Frank said Joey was doing okay, as long as you didn't ask him to do anything really complicated or try to have a deep conversation with him.

She found Joey mucking out Harlequin's stall. The boy was tall and thin, dressed in baggy pants and a plaid flannel shirt that was surely too warm for the weather. His outfit was topped off with a baseball cap, worn backwards in spite of the bright sunlight. He was also wearing headphones for a Walkman.

It was really kind of comical to watch because Joey was not only raking, he was dancing as well. He'd drag a little straw in time to the music no one else could hear. Then he'd hold up the rake like a mock guitar, playing the metal tines with an imaginary pick. Samantha thought it was like watching television with the sound off.

"Hi Joey," she called. "I'm Samantha."

The young man paid no attention but just kept rocking back and forth with his rake. She called again with the same results. Finally, in frustration, she walked right up in front of his face and pulled one earpiece aside.

"Hi. I'm Samantha."

Startled, Joey retorted, "Well, you don't have to yell."

"Sorry," said the girl with an apologetic grin. "I'm Frank's daughter."

Joey sized her up. "I don't think so. Frank said he had a little girl." He put his headphones back in place and went on raking and rolling.

"No, Joey, wait," Samantha protested. She tapped him on the shoulder, and he slid the headphones down onto his neck. He looked irritated. "I really am Frank's little girl. Look. See. Here's my I.D. It says I'm Samantha Kelly and has my picture."

"Oh." Joey acknowledged her card. "I got one of those too," He indicated the card that was snapped onto his shirt pocket. "Can't get in without it."

Wanting to change the subject, Samantha asked, "Where's Harlequin?"

"Some guy took him over to McCauley's barn," Joey answered. "I don't usually let anyone touch Frank's horses, but the guy said he was Doctor Something or Other, so I let the horse go. I don't like doctors much."

So the owners are bailing on my dad already. Sadly, she noticed that several other stall guards were also hanging loose, the stalls behind them empty.

Joey started to put his headphones back on when he suddenly changed his mind. "Where is Frank anyway? I didn't get my check yesterday."

"Oh, sorry," Samantha said, hastily pulling the folded envelope out of her back pocket and handing it to him. She decided not to try to explain about her dad. "My dad's – uh – away for a couple of days. He sent me here to help you and Uncle Jack."

Joey's eyes lit up when he took the check. "Thanks! I was getting pretty broke, and I want to go over to the midway tonight and get high."

When Samantha noted his comment and looked suspiciously at him out of the corner of her eye, he laughed and said, "on the Ferris wheel. You know, like *high* up in the air. " He laughed again, fully enjoying his little attempt at humor.

Chug, who had heard Samantha's voice, started acting up in his stall.

"Hang on, Chug. I'm coming," she called to the colt. Turning to the groom, she said, "I'm going to take the colt to the track. Will you help me tack him up?"

"Sure, Samantha," Joey answered, leaning the rake inside the empty stall.

He followed her into the tack room at the end of the barn and took a lead rope off a hook on the wall. "I'll go get him."

Samantha glanced around, a little amazed at how orderly everything was. She had to admit that the tack room had never been so tidy, even when she took care of it. She noticed a neatly made cot in the corner. Joey had tacked a picture of his parents and himself over his bed, and there were a couple of books on the crate that served as a nightstand next to the bed. She could see that Joey took his new job very seriously.

She found her safety helmet and vest and slipped them on. Hooking a bridle over her shoulder, she picked up a flat saddle from a rack on the wall, stuck a short riding crop into her back pocket and went to find Joey and her horse. She smiled broadly. She could hardly wait to ride Chug again.

When she got her first glimpse of the colt in the morning sunlight, it almost took her breath away. He was spectacular! Once again, he was Sierra Warrior, not the gangly little colt she had named Chuggy. Joey was patting the colt and talking to him. She liked that.

When the horse was saddled and bridled, she gave him an affectionate hug. His mane was soft and silky, and he smelled clean and fresh like a combination of shampoo and new alfalfa hay. It was a remembered smell she always loved.

Joey gave her a leg up and cautioned, "Be careful, Samantha. There's some really strange people around here these days." She thought that was kind of weird, but maybe he'd seen the old cowboy too. Briefly, she considered quizzing him, but Joey had already returned to his work. She clucked to Chug and he danced forward, eager to get to work.

As she rounded the corner and headed for the track, she saw Wilma Youngman riding Red, her big red and white Appaloosa pony horse. She was leading an unsaddled gray Thoroughbred, and the bells on her tack jingled as she rode. Samantha smiled as she observed the sturdy Appaloosa. Some non-track people didn't understand that pony horses or lead ponies were just any kind of horse used to accompany or "pony" racehorses to the track. No one, however, could ever mistake Red for a pony in the usual sense.

Wilma was an old family friend and she called out to Samantha. "Ride with me, honey. No one'll bother you if we're together."

"Thanks, Wilma." She urged Chug up on the other side of Wilma's gelding.

"How've you been, all things considered?" the older woman asked kindly. The girl basked momentarily in the warmth of the big woman's smile. Wilma was part of that extended racetrack family she had always enjoyed. Mrs. Wilson had made her feel like an outsider, but Wilma's friendly welcome made her feel much better.

"We're hanging in there," Samantha sighed.

"Well, don't you worry, honey," the big woman assured her. "Most of us don't believe all that nonsense they're saying about your dad. And, like I always say, anything that doesn't kill you, makes you stronger."

Samantha wished she had Wilma's easygoing disposition. Not much worried her friend. She made a joke out of practically everything and laughed heartily, sometimes even at herself. Once, when she had first gotten Red, she had caught the reflection of herself riding the horse as they passed the track kitchen window.

"Well, I'll be danged," she had laughed. "I've finally got a horse with a rear end as big as mine!" Samantha and her father hadn't dared to look at each other for fear they might laugh too.

"Oh, get real, you two," Wilma had said. "You know it's true."

"Aw, Wilma, you're just fishing for compliments," Frank Kelly had said with a barely-concealed laugh as he kicked the horse he was riding up past her.

Samantha smiled as Wilma jogged alongside her, chatting merrily, bells jingling. Just as they were getting ready to enter the track, she heard Jeff call out. "Samantha, wait."

When he reached the two riders, he said, "Look, coming down the stretch."

Galloping toward them was a big black and white Appaloosa. With every stride, Samantha could hear the rhythmical "huff, huff" of his breath as his front feet hit the ground. It was Chug, but it wasn't Chug. It was Warhawk, and he was as dazzling as his brother. Chug gave a start, wanting to join the fun. When Samantha reined him back, he backed up six quick steps and danced in place. "Easy, boy," she said, holding the big colt in check.

"Well, I'll be danged!" Wilma swore. "They're identical."

"Not quite," Jeff explained. "Warhawk's got a white sock. Otherwise, you're right. They do look alike."

"Won't that track announcer have his eyes full when those two run together!" Wilma chuckled.

"If they ever run together," Slade said, walking up behind the group. "He's gotta have a trainer first."

"Ignore that little cuss," Wilma said to Samantha under her breath and started onto the track. "Come on, Sam, we've got work to do."

Undaunted by Wilma's comments, Slade just grinned and waited for Warhawk to return.

"Somebody ought to lock that ornery kid up," Wilma said as they jogged past the grandstand where the usual group of railbirds - people who watch the morning workouts - had their stopwatches out to gather a little betting background for upcoming races. And there he was with the others, the old cowboy with the gray beard and the cane.

"Wilma," Samantha asked, "do you know who that old guy with the gray beard is?"

The older woman tried to get a good look as they jogged past the watchers. "Can't say as I do, but he walked by me a little while ago, and he smells like he hasn't had a bath in a month."

Samantha turned to look back. There was something vaguely familiar about the man, but she just couldn't put her finger on it. In the bright morning sunlight, he didn't look quite as threatening as he had the previous night in the dark. *Probably some old trainer I used to know who hasn't been around for a long time, she thought. Or maybe it's--her* heart skipped a beat for just a second – *no, it couldn't be – too senior, too short, and too sloppy.*

Frank Kelly was in his mid thirties, tall, broad-shouldered and a sharp dresser. In fact, everyone wondered how anyone who worked with horses for a living could be so neat all the time. This guy was wearing dingy, wrinkled clothes that looked like he had slept in them for a week. *Definitely not my dad.* She turned back to Wilma.

"I think I'll breeze Chug a little," Samantha said to her friend. She kicked the colt into an easy lope, leaving Wilma behind.

The horse traveled effortlessly over the track. Samantha found herself thinking *this is the way racing really is – the breeze in your face, a good horse, and no need to think about anything but what you're doing right now.*

She urged the horse a little faster and she could tell, even then, that he still had a lot of speed and stamina in reserve and would deliver it when called on to run. She crouched low in the saddle and opened him up for about a quarter of a mile, thoroughly enjoying the exhilarating ride. "Woo-hoo!" she shouted. "That's my boy!"

When she got back to the barns, Joey was waiting to unsaddle and cool out the colt. Samantha jumped down, feeling energized and happy in spite of everything. She gave Chug's sweaty neck a big hug and handed him over to Joey.

"I saw that red-headed kid following you over to the track," Joey offered quietly as he pulled Chug's saddle off. "Better stay away from him. He's mean."

Well, that's the second time in an hour someone has told me Slade Lang is mean. I've known that for years. Guess everybody is finally on to his tricks.

"What makes you think he's mean?" she asked the groom.

"I dunno," Joey answered. "He's just sneaky, and he gives me the creeps. I see him sometimes at night prowling around the barns when no one else is here. What's that all about anyway?"

Samantha put the saddle on a rack in the tack room and turned to answer Joey, but he had already led Chug over to the hot walker at the other end of the barn. Her joyful expression turned suddenly serious when she realized it was time to go over to the California Horse Racing Board office.

*   *   *

The small office was crowded with owners, trainers, jockeys, and a few journalists and photographers with cameras hanging around their necks. Samantha took her place in line and began to read their mission statement that was in a frame on the wall just inside the door.

"The purpose of the California Horse Racing Board is to regulate pari-mutuel wagering for the protection of the betting public, to promote horse racing and breeding industries, and to maximize State of California tax revenues."

Frank had told Samantha that the CHRB had been formed back in the 1930s to supervise the state's racing activities and enforce racing rules. All of the stewards and judges reported to the board, and everyone who conducted any kind of business at the track had to have a CHRB license. They also collected the state's share of monies wagered during race meets. Like the other race trackers, the board employees traveled from fair to fair, setting up their office as each new meet began.

When it was Samantha's turn, she greeted Betty, the clerk, with a friendly smile and asked about her father in a quiet voice. She thought maybe it was just her imagination, but the room seemed suddenly very still, like everyone was listening. She felt her face getting red.

Betty cleared her throat nervously and then politely refused to discuss the case with her. Samantha had known Betty for years and expected her to help, but the older woman remained firm and businesslike. She could not give out any information.

"Say hi to your mom for me," Betty called as Samantha turned to leave.

"Yeah, right," Samantha mumbled under her breath. She might have gotten somewhere if she'd tried pleading and little-girl tears, but that wasn't Samantha's style. She just got her back up and huffed out the door. Totally, discouraged, she headed for home.

Chapter VII

WINNERS AT THE FAIR

When Samantha arrived back at the trailer, she was disappointed to find that Uncle Jack was nowhere to be seen. There were still a lot of unanswered questions. She was wondering where she might find him when she spied a note lying folded on the table. Opening it quickly, she wondered what kind of excuse Uncle Jack had this time. The note said:

Nice work, Sam. Just gallop him the rest of the week. Don't worry, Love, Dad.

Her heart leaped! He was here! Somewhere! Where? Finally, she had some hope that things were going to be all right. She put two fingers to her lips and then placed a kiss on Chug's picture. "All right!"

It had gotten warm early that morning, and Samantha was feeling really sticky. Quickly, she showered, put on some clean clothes and braided her still-wet hair. She just had to tell someone about the note from her dad. She knew Tracy's mother still wouldn't welcome her, so she headed for Ida Mae's.

"Ida Mae! Ida Mae!" Samantha called, knocking repeatedly on the screen door. Each bang echoed twice as the door hit the jam.

"Come in, come in," came the friendly reply, and Samantha entered the coach just in time to see Ida Mae take a big batch of blueberry muffins out of the oven. The aroma brought a noisy complaint from her stomach, but she was determined to ignore it for a moment.

"He's here, Ida Mae!" she exclaimed. "My dad's here!"

"Well, of course he is," Ida Mae, said without surprise. "Sit down and have something to eat, and we'll talk about it."

Samantha slid into the dinette, and Ida Mae turned the hot muffins out onto a clean dishtowel on the table. She added a tub of butter and a couple of glasses of milk.

Samantha slathered butter on one of the muffins, jiggling it around in her hands because it was still piping hot. She took a little bite, burned her tongue and reached for the milk.

"He left me a note," she said, taking another careful bite and talking with her mouth full, which would have scandalized her mother.

"Well, darlin', he never actually left," Ida Mae explained. "He's been bunking with us for the past couple of days, but he can't let anyone see him because he's been nosing around, trying to find out who the real culprit is. Of course, he won't be staying here anymore now that you're here. That way you can honestly say you don't know where he is if anyone asks. Your dad still has a lot of friends on the circuit, and we all plan to support him until this whole thing blows over."

Samantha knew her father had helped some of the trainers who were down on their luck. Maybe it was payback time.

"McCauley's taken Harlequin D," Ida Mae continued.

Well, that explains why the big leopard is gone. What a relief!

"And Tommy and I are gonna train Sierra Maiden and the Graingers' two geldings. Jerry's agreed to take Little Sis and Mountain Dew. I think Shorty Simmons will get the other three. That just leaves Chug, and he doesn't need a race until Vallejo or

Santa Rosa. We're not gonna let this thing put your dad out of business. He's our friend."

"How can we ever thank you, Ida Mae? Samantha asked, feeling truly warm and safe for the first time since she'd returned to the track. The Kellys still had their extended track family, and they were all rallying around them.

"Fiddlesticks," said the older woman, polishing off her third muffin. "What are friends for anyway?"

Samantha started on her second muffin. They were delicious, and she had been hungrier than she realized. Also, knowing that her father was near, even if she couldn't be with him, was a comfort.

"Now that you've got that off your mind," Ida Mae went on, "want to go over and look at the arts and crafts at the fair with me? I entered an afghan, and they were going to be judging this morning."

*   *   *

Ten minutes later, they were happy to duck into the cool, quiet atmosphere of the big exhibition hall in the center of the fairgrounds. Samantha led the way over to where the quilts were hanging all along the east wall. She loved quilts, and there were some spectacular ones in the display. Of course, she thought the ones Grandma made were better, but some of the prettier ones might run a close second.

From quilts, they turned to examine the little groupings of handcrafts in the center of the hall. When Samantha saw a display of models of the twenty-one Calfornia missions, it brought back memories of the fourth grade when all California school children study the Spanish Mission Period.

"I made one like this." She pointed to a small replica of Mission San Gabriel. "Only mine wasn't this good. My buildings looked more like chicken coops than churches. I did write a pretty good poem describing the bell tower though."

They were walking by an exhibit of American Indian handwork when a beautiful fringed deerskin shirt caught Samantha's eye. The shirt was an amazing piece of work, decorated with hand-sewn beads and colored porcupine quills. There were moccasins to match. She was pleasantly surprised when she read the name of the craftsman on the card.

"It's Wilma's!" she exclaimed. "And, she's won the blue ribbon!"

"Well, I'll be," said Ida Mae in amazement. "Imagine Wilma sitting still long enough to make something as beautiful as that. I guess now we know what she does in the evenings."

Somehow it was hard to imagine the six-foot horsewoman doing such delicate work, but Samantha did know that Wilma was at least one-fourth American Indian. Wilma had said that her folks came from Montana and that their last name "Youngman" had originally been two words.

"Wait 'til Wilma sees this," Ida Mae beamed, truly happy for their friend. "She'll be proud as a peacock."

They found the afghans in the far north corner of the hall, artfully draped over chairs and cedar chests that had been crafted by local high school students. An intricately patterned red, white and blue one immediately jumped out at Samantha. She knew it just had to be Ida Mae's.

"I got a blue too!" Ida Mae exclaimed with delight as she spotted her work. Samantha could tell she was genuinely pleased.

And also proud as a peacock.

"My grandma would be so tickled," Ida Mae said. "She spent a lot of time teaching me to crochet."

"But it's your work," Samantha added, happy to have such a talented friend. "Besides, good people have magic, and you're good people."

"Oh, darlin', I love you for that!" She hugged Samantha and wiped away a few loose tears. "We've got to celebrate. How about a turkey leg from Bubba's?"

"That would be awesome," said the girl, remembering turkey leg feasts at Bubba's little restaurant from previous years at this fair.

On their way out, they stopped at a 4-H exhibit near the door.

"Did you know that our horse racing helps pay for 4-H?" Ida Mae asked. Samantha shook her head. "Yep. Part of every dollar people bet at the track goes back to the state, and they use it to promote agriculture and help 4-H and Future Farmers of America."

Samantha was in FFA and had been a 4-Her, but she hadn't known about the racing connection. "Well, that's good to know," she said. She tucked the information away to use as a possible report next year at school.

When they stepped out of the door, a blast of hot air almost took Samantha's breath away. Heat radiated up from the blacktop, and she felt her feet getting hot right through her tennis shoes. She began to sweat.

No. Horses sweat, men perspire, and ladies feel the heat, her mother always said. Well, she was feeling the heat in spades today.

On the way to Bubba's, they passed vendors selling everything from cotton candy to cowboy hats. Samantha greeted some of the regular sellers she had known for a long time. "Got a horse for me today, Sam?" some would ask.

"Yeah, try Roy Rogers on Trigger in the seventh," was her standard answer.

Larry Ogden, who had been selling corn dogs ever since Samantha could remember, told her that Jorge had told him to bet on Cherry Blossom in the third.

Samantha and Ida Mae looked at each other with a grin. "I don't think so," the girl said. "The Tylers are gonna win that one."

"But Jorge's a jockey," Larry protested.

"They're the worst ones to listen to," Ida Mae said with a laugh. "They all think they're going to win, but only one gets the trophy."

"The *Racing Form* likes that horse," Larry continued. "Her works have been good."

"Well," Ida Mae admitted. "She's our toughest competition in this race, but I think we can beat her."

Larry pulled out a racing program and hastily scribbled something on it. "I'll keep that in mind, Ida Mae," he said with a smile. "Meanwhile, how about a corn dog?"

"No thanks," said Samantha. "We are just dying for one of Bubba's turkey legs."

"Can't say as I blame you," Larry admitted with a sigh as Samantha and Ida Mae took their leave.

Ida Mae pulled Samantha over to a booth where they were selling oversized, foam rubber cowboy hats. "Wouldn't James just love this!" she exclaimed.

"Oh, yeah," Samantha answered, remembering how her little brother liked to show off, sometimes to her great embarrassment. "I'll have to get him one before we leave."

They stopped for a while to enjoy the shade in a small park area where wrought-iron benches surrounded a little pavilion.

"I can't believe this heat," Ida Mae said as she flopped down on one of the nearby benches.

"Me neither," Samantha answered. "I don't remember it being so hot here last year."

"I don't think it was," Ida Mae speculated. "Stockton's hot and Pomona's hot, but Pleasanton has always been pretty mild this time of year."

Up on the stage, a petite blonde girl about Samantha's age was belting out *Your Cheatin' Heart* accompanied by a Karaoke system. The girl was putting her whole heart and soul into the song, and Samantha found herself wishing she could sing that well. Uncle Jack was good, and so was her mother, but Samantha didn't have any confidence in her voice at all. Sometimes, though, her poetry made her heart sing.

"Woo-hoo!" Ida Mae cheered. "I just love that real country music. She pulled a dollar out of the pocket of her Levis and put it into a glass at the foot of the stage as they walked by. "Come on, girl," she said to Samantha. "Let's go get some real country food to go with this great music."

*   *   *

Half an hour later as Ida Mae was cleaning off her face and hands with a wet wipe, she looked at her watch and said, "Well, that turkey was flat delicious, but I've got to run. It's almost time for the third race, and Tommy's gonna need me."

"I'll help saddle," Samantha offered.

"Well, aren't you a sweetheart!" It was really a statement rather than a question. Ida Mae gave the girl an affectionate hug. "Let's go then."

Chapter VIII

GALADRIEL

Samantha and Ida Mae chatted happily as they walked along the dusty path from the barns to the racetrack. It had gotten hotter – the weatherman had said the mercury was likely to top the 100-degree mark. Samantha would have been worried about racing a horse today except for the fact that she knew a four and one-half furlong race lasted less than a minute.

The horse Ida Mae was leading was a two-year-old Appaloosa filly named Galadriel – Ida Mae was big on Tolkien and *Lord of the Rings*. She had raised the filly on the Tyler ranch near Tucson where they spent their winters. At the barn, Tommy had been kidding his wife about how she babied the spotted filly too much, but Samantha had stood up for her friend. She understood how fond Ida Mae was of the horse; she felt the same way about Chug.

When they got to the receiving barn, Samantha spotted Chris Lathrop, the track identifier, whom she had known for years. His job was to check the filly against the description on her papers and look at the numbers tattooed inside her upper lip.

Samantha greeted Chris with a bright smile. "Hey, Chris," but he just busied himself with his job and totally ignored her.

She pretended not to notice the slight, but it hurt nonetheless. She was getting sick of people who were supposed to be her friends not being friendly or even polite. She followed Ida Mae into the saddling paddock where Tommy was waiting in stall three where they would saddle the filly. Their jockey, Pat Carillo, was already there. He managed a weak "Hi," but he seemed a little embarrassed to see Samantha also. She wanted to shout to the entire world, "My dad never hurt Pinky's horse!" but she knew it was useless at this point.

Pat was wearing the Tyler racing silks that were deep blue with yellow stars. Ida Mae called them her "Tolkien wizard colors."

Unmindful of what other people might think, Tommy Tyler gave Samantha a big hug and said, "Glad you're here, Sugar," which made her feel a whole lot better.

After the horses were saddled, the grooms began to walk them around the paddock. Owners and bettors crowded the short fence surrounding the saddling area to watch their favorites and size up their chances. One was marking something down on his race program with a stubby golf pencil. Another had his form out and was reading with his finger following the lines of print. A young woman was snapping pictures.

As the horses circled, some, like Galadriel led by Ida Mae, were calm. Others danced at the ends of their leads. One bay gelding was lathered all over. Grandpa Kelly would have said the *washy* horse had already run its race in the paddock and didn't have much left for the actual competition.

"Jockeys up!" the paddock judge called sharply, and Tommy gave Pat a leg up on Galadriel.

"Remember, hold her in until you get to the head of the stretch," were his final instructions to the jockey. At the gate, he mounted his pony horse and led Galadriel out onto the track behind the number one and number two horses. The rest of the field followed in numerical order. Samantha heard the trumpeter play the call to post, and the horses began to file past the grandstand.

The post parade allowed people in the stands to see each horse and match it up with the numbers on the program. That way, they would know who owned, who trained, and who rode each horse. Samantha smiled. Once again, the colorful Appaloosas brought a lot of "oohs" an "ahs" from the spectators.

"Hey, Sam," Wilma called as she jingled past leading the number eight horse. "Did you see my blue ribbon?"

"You bet!" returned the girl, holding two thumbs up. "Awesome!"

"Come on, darlin', let's go get a good spot on the rail," Ida Mae urged.

"I want to get a program," said the girl. "I'll meet you over there."

"I'll be close to the winner's circle," Ida Mae said with a wink.

A few minutes later, Samantha squeezed in next to her friend and began to read the information about the horses in the third race. It was a maiden race, for horses that hadn't yet had a win. She looked across the infield and spotted the starting gate. On the big screen television above the tote board, she could see the horses and their pony riders leisurely moving toward it. The walk would take about 10 minutes, giving fairgoers time to place their bets.

Samantha found herself thinking this would have been the perfect race for Chug since some of these horses were also paid into the Cal-Bred. But, there would be other races, and she was thankful her horse wasn't going to have to run in this heat.

"The horses are at the gate," came the announcer's voice over the public address system. Samantha took a deep breath. The bell rang. "They're running!"

Trying to spot Ida Mae's filly, Samantha strained her eyes as the horses streaked toward the turn, but the field was just a big blur of blacks and bays and spots.

"Coming up to the turn, it's Heavenly Angel and Cherry Blossom," came the call.

"Hold her back, Pat. Just wait," Ida Mae was mumbling under her breath.

"As they round the turn, it's Heavenly Angel and Cherry Blossom, with Cat Dancing, followed by Galadriel. Chance's Choice and War Chief are together in fifth, with Melanie's Girl and Lancer trailing the pack.

"Around the turn, it's Heavenly Angel and Cherry Blossom. War Chief is moving up on the outside to claim third with Galadriel running fourth."

"Now!" shouted Ida Mae, and Samantha watched Pat steer the filly through a hole between Cherry Blossom and War Chief.

"And Galadriel moves up to second!" shouted the announcer as caught up in the close race as everyone else. "Down the stretch, it's Heavenly Angel and Galadriel in second. Now, Galadriel takes the lead! And here comes Cherry Blossom on the rail, but she can't catch Galadriel."

"Come on, baby girl!" Ida Mae shouted, jumping up and down.

"It's Galadriel by a head!" came the final call as the horses crossed the wire. Ida Mae whooped.

"I knew she could do it. Come on, darlin'. Let's go get our picture taken."

The tote board showed Galadriel, Cherry Blossom and Heavenly Angel running one, two, three, but then the "Inquiry" sign lit up.

"Hold all tickets, folks. We've got an inquiry," said the announcer, and the crowd gave a collective groan.

Ida Mae and Samantha waited in the winner's circle as Pat brought Galadriel slowly down the track and walked her back and forth, waiting for the judges' ruling. The filly was breathing hard and dripping with sweat. Nearby, Jake Lang, who was Cherry Blossom's trainer, also waited for the final ruling.

"What happened?" Ida Mae asked her husband.

"Aw, Jake says Pat hit his jockey with a whip as they were coming down the stretch," Tommy answered with disgust. "You know Pat wouldn't do that."

Samantha watched as Slade walked his dad's horse back and forth on the track near Galadriel, a smug smile on his face. She glanced up toward the booth at the top of the grandstand where the judges were viewing film of the race. In just a few minutes, the inquiry sign went off, and the places were left where they were.

"There will be no change in the order of finish, folks," came the announcement. Jake Lang's complaint had been disallowed. The winners cheered; the losers grumbled and tore up their tickets.

Pat steered Galadriel into the winner's circle, and they all lined up on either side of the filly for the win picture. Samantha could see Jake Lang gesturing angrily at his son as they led Cherry Blossom toward the barns, but she was determined not to think about what he might be saying.

A few minutes later, the Tylers led the sweaty filly to the test barn where officials would take urine samples from the first three horses to make certain no illegal medications were used on the horses during the race. Samantha noticed that Galadriel's muscles were starting to twitch. She was still dripping wet and looked a little wild-eyed like she was afraid of something.

Concerned, Ida Mae hustled the filly back toward the barns. Samantha touched Galadriel's sweaty flank. It was so hot she unconsciously jerked her hand back. The horse stumbled twice, and Ida Mae frowned, said "Easy Baby," and kept her moving. When they reached the Tyler barn, Tommy grabbed a hose and started a cool stream of water over the horse's back. The filly shivered.

"Ida Mae, go get Doc," he directed. "Sam, run to the kitchen and get all the ice you can carry."

When Samantha returned, her arms aching from the cold ice, the Tylers and the vet were inside Galadriel's stall. The filly was down and her breathing was labored. The muscles all over her body were twitching constantly. Ida Mae cradled the filly's head on her lap. She talked softly and stroked Galadriel's head. The woman's tears flowed freely.

Samantha dropped the ice bags near the vet and backed into a corner of the stall. She wanted to run away because she had never seen a horse in such distress before, but she didn't want to desert her friends. She just stood there frozen, a look of horror on her face. She felt her lunch wanting to come up and swallowed hard.

Tommy and the vet packed the ice all around the horse's head in a last-ditch attempt to save her life, but their efforts were useless. It was all over in a few minutes.

Samantha knew she would never forget the scene before her. She had never watched a horse die before today. Oh, she'd seen a few dead calves at Grandpa's dairy, but they were already stiff and somehow didn't look real. This was real, and it was awful. Her throat ached with wanting to cry. From

93

faraway, she could hear the music of the midway. It sounded suddenly raucous and off-key.

She knew she had to get out of there before she made a blubbering fool of herself. The Tylers didn't need a crybaby on their hands right now. Tommy was hugging Ida Mae, and the people standing at the stall entrance were all offering their condolences. They didn't notice Samantha slipping out between them.

Running blindly, she turned the corner at the end of the shed row and smacked right into the old cowboy, almost knocking him off his feet.

"Easy there, youngin'," he cautioned in a croaky voice, groaning as he bent over with difficulty to retrieve his cane. He put his right hand behind his back as if to straighten up his spine, then snugged his sunglasses back into place. She could see leftovers from lunch on his beard. "What's got you so fired up anyway?" As he stretched out a grubby hand toward her, Samantha ducked out of his reach.

"Leave me alone, and quit following me!" she shouted, making a beeline for home. *I don't care if that guy is one of Dad's old friends. He smells bad and he gives me the creeps.*

As she ran, thoughts like "why do bad things happen to good people?" crowded her mind. Ida Mae and Tommy didn't deserve this and neither did the filly.

At the coach, she kicked the door three times and cussed when her trembling fingers couldn't get the key into the lock. Finally inside, she kicked off her shoes, climbed up to her bed and lay there, staring at the ceiling.

She wanted to cry, but the tears just wouldn't come. She kept wondering if horses went to heaven when they died. She knew it was a childish thought, but right now, she didn't feel like she wanted to be grown up anymore.

And then, she did what she always did when she was especially happy or sad. She went into the kitchen, turned on the laptop and started to write.

Farewell, Galadriel
Run sure and swift, my spotted friend.
Kick up your heels and flee!
Cast off your reins and bridle.
Go quickly now; you're free!

And as you travel through the mists,
Heed not the sound of tears.
'Tis just the westwind at your back,
That whispers in your ears.

Rest safe beneath green willows,
And when the morning's nigh,
Take time to taste the crystal spring
Beneath the warm, blue sky.

Old friends are in yon meadow.
In fun they'll spend the day.
Pray join them; they are waiting,
To share their carefree play.

We'll miss you, not forget you,
Though in time our grief will pass.
Your deeds will linger in our hearts,
My beautiful, brave lass.

It took the girl almost two hours to write the poem, and by the time she had composed the last two lines, tears were flowing freely. She wiped her nose with the back of her hand, hit the print button and went into the bathroom to get some Kleenex. She was blowing her nose hard when Uncle Jack came in.

"Sam?" he called.

"In here, Uncle Jack," she sniffed. She went into the kitchen.

"I heard about Ida Mae's filly," he said softly. He held out his arms to comfort his niece, but Samantha knew a hug would only make her start crying again.

"I wrote a poem," she sniffled and dabbed at her red-rimmed eyes with the Kleenex. She handed the paper to her uncle.

As he finished reading it, he blinked back a tear. "You need to give this to Ida Mae."

"You really like it?"

"Absolutely. It's your very best."

A few minutes later, she found Ida Mae in her kitchen baking brownies.

"I bake when I'm happy, and I bake when I'm sad," the older woman said with a weak attempt at humor. Her eyes were swollen and red.

"I write," Samantha said, shyly offering the poem to her friend.

Ida Mae began to read. Her hands were shaking as she read the last line. "Why, darlin', this is the nicest thing anyone has ever done for me. I'm so glad I have you for a friend."

"Me too," Samantha answered as they hugged through bittersweet tears.

Chapter IX

UNCLE BILLY NORTON

Lost in thought, as she made her way slowly and sadly back to her father's coach, she didn't notice when Slade Lang fell in step beside her.

"Well, that's one more Cal-Bred out of the race," he hissed.

Startled, Samantha jumped. Then, she clenched her fists and gritted her teeth, wanting so much to punch him right in his freckled, pimpled face.

"We have to be nice to the Lang boys…" was all that kept her from taking her best shot. She kept going, but Slade was still dogging her tracks.

"And your family always seems to be right in the middle of it," he taunted.

"That's it!" Samantha stopped and faced the older boy, her green eyes blazing, her fists clinched so hard her nails bit into her palms. "My dad never drugged Pinky's horse!"

"Yeah, I know," Slade, admitted grudgingly. "He's too much of a goody-goody to do anything like that."

Samantha relaxed a little.

"But what about your uncle?" he suggested with a half smile and a raised eyebrow. "Everyone knows he owes those casino men a lot of money."

"You really are nasty, aren't you?" she countered, her Irish riled up to a new high. "What about your dad and that phony inquiry he filed today?"

"It wasn't phony," Slade protested. "I saw Pat whack our jockey."

"You never did," the girl answered in disgust. "Pat Carillo doesn't do that kind of stuff. Only someone who would could think he might."

"I know what I saw." Slade refused to give in.

"Oh, get a life, Slade," Samantha said. She turned and walked away.

If he comes after me, I'm gonna slug him. She pounded her right fist into her left hand and looked over her shoulder, but she wasn't being followed.

Unfortunately, what Slade had said about Uncle Jack had sparked up just the teeniest bit of doubt that had already been nagging at the back of her mind. She knew her uncle liked to gamble. That was why he had left his job as a bartender in Reno and moved to the Kelly ranch in Southern California to work last winter. She also knew he had been in Reno a few weeks ago, and it sounded like he had run up a considerable gambling tab. The night he had been drinking, he had said they took his whole paycheck. He also mumbled something about doing what they asked. *But drug a horse? No way.* She vowed to grill him as soon as she got home, but a call from Tracy interrupted her thoughts.

"Hey, Sam," said the girl, "Uncle Billy's back. Want to go see him?"

Samantha stopped and let her friend catch up.

"Sure, why not," Samantha answered without enthusiasm. "I could use some laughs right now. My life feels totally trashed." But as she was feeling really sorry for herself, she suddenly realized that the bad things that had happened recently hadn't really happened to her at all. Pinky's horse had been drugged, and Ida Mae had lost her beautiful filly, and her dad had been accused of a terrible crime. Nothing at all had really happened directly to her.

Stop feeling sorry for yourself, Samantha Kelly. But she still found herself wishing things would get back to normal. Maybe she would wake up and this would all be a bad dream. *Oh, get real!*

"Let's go, Trace," she said. "I haven't seen Uncle Billy since last year."

Uncle Billy Norton was a retired racetrack trainer and something of legend with racing folk. Over 80, he still showed up at every meet, "just to keep you boys honest," he always said. He was a favorite with everybody because he had rubbed elbows with movie stars like Bing Crosby and Desi Arnaz way back in the 1940s and 1950s. His list of friends and acquaintances was like a Who's Who of horse racing and movie stars. He'd even watched Seabiscuit run, knew his trainer and all. Uncle Billy's racing stories always drew a crowd, and today was no different.

When the two girls arrived at the track kitchen, they found Uncle Billy seated on a picnic table outside. Surrounded by racing people of all ages, he was just finishing up one of his stories.

Another year had rounded the big man out a bit, and his hair gleamed white in the afternoon sunlight, but his blue eyes still had the old Norton twinkle Samantha loved.

"And that's exactly how it happened," he said with a laugh that was echoed by his audience. He saw the two girls and motioned them to come up and sit beside him.

"Oh, if I was just ten years younger," he said with an exaggerated sigh. "You two fillies have just grown up fine. Makes my old heart go pitter-patter." He patted his chest with both hands fluttering, a charming little-boy grin on his face. Samantha suddenly felt hot, and she knew she was turning red. She hated to be the center of attention. Not so Tracy; she loved it.

"Shame on you, Uncle Billy," Tracy teased back. "You're old enough to be my father."

"Heck, I'm old enough to be your great-grandpa," he replied with another big laugh.

"Tell us another story, Uncle Billy," someone called.

He thought for a moment and said, "Did I ever tell you about the time we stole the pony horse?"

Everyone said, "No," and he started his story.

"Well, as I recall, it was about 1948 over at Stockton. I know it was the first meet of the season anyway. Chuck Larsen had this really wild colt that he couldn't get broke. The rank S.O.B. just flat tried to kill anyone in the vicinity too. In desperation one day, Chuck hooks the horse up to his pickup and starts dragging him around the barns. The horse was pitching a hissy fit, and he slipped and fell down. Skinned up his head a might.

"Unfortunately, Marty Rogers, who didn't have much use for Chuck anyway, just happened to see the whole thing. He reported Chuck to the Humane Society, and they fined him $500. That was a lot of money in those days."

Some of Uncle Billy's older listeners nodded their heads in agreement. Five hundred dollars was several month's pay during the Great Depression.

"Anyhow, Chuck fumed about it for days. If he saw Marty, he'd walk in the other direction, and all in all, he had a pretty bad meet. He blamed Marty for everything that went wrong, too. For weeks, nobody wanted to be around Chuck because he was such a grouch.

"On getaway day, Marty comes up to me and asks me to take his pony horse to the auction because it had broke down and wasn't worth hauling to the next fair. I said I would, and then I got this great idea."

Uncle Billy grinned like a little kid about to raid the cookie jar.

"I found Chuck packing to leave and told him that Marty had left, but that he had forgotten his pony. 'Wanna take him over to the auction and sell him?' I asked Chuck. His old eyes lit up for the first time in weeks, and he grinned in anticipation of getting even, rubbing his hands together like the villain in an old silent movie. I could hardly keep a straight face.

"So we loaded up the broken-down pony and hauled him off. They give us 20 bucks, which I gave Chuck. And to this day, that ole boy still thinks he got even with Marty by stealing his pony horse."

Everyone laughed and clapped. "What happened to the rank S.O.B.?" Tracy asked. Uncle Billy took a long drink from his water bottle.

"You know, Sis, he turned out to be one of the top runners of the year. Chuck made a lot of money with him. Guess the truck training kind of cured him, but I wouldn't recommend it."

"Tell us another story, Uncle Billy," another listener called. The trainer took another drink of water.

"The one about catching the grain thief," Samantha suggested. She had heard it before, but it got better with each telling.

"It was back in the 1930s during the Depression," Uncle Billy began. "I was just a kid, of course. Everybody was broke except for a few top trainers who had movie star owners and such. I was lucky enough to have an owner who was doing better than most, and we had plenty of feed for ourselves and the horses – but no extra.

"I was doing the feeding myself in those days, and I kept noticing my grain barrel going down faster than it should, considering the number of horses I had at the time. I watched and I waited. I posted someone else to watch when I couldn't, but the grain just kept disappearing. We just couldn't figure out who was taking it and how.

"Then, one night, I decided to park myself in the tack room all night and get to the bottom of the mystery. I hid in a corner right next to the grain barrel, and I had a flashlight so I could surprise whoever was doing the pilfering.

"I was close to falling asleep when I heard a slight scratching noise on the outside of the wall. The moon was out, so I could see a little without turning on the flashlight. I watched as slowly and quietly, a board behind the grain barrel slid to one side. Then, a little bitty kid, no more'n five or six squeezed through the opening into the tack room. I could barely see him in the moonlight, but I did see he had a three-pound coffee can with him. He dipped it into the barrel and handed it back through the hole in the wall. Another can appeared, and he filled that one too. That's when I grabbed him by the leg.

"Well, he let out such a stream of cuss words I just about fell over laughing. Here's this little thing, no bigger than a minute, and he knew more cuss words than a sixty-year-old sailor. It was the funniest thing I ever saw! I reached over to get the flashlight, and he called me ' a big…' Well, we won't go there with the ladies present. That made me laugh even harder."

Samantha could just picture the big man doubled over with glee.

"While I was rocking with laughter and wiping my eyes, he pulled loose and skittered back out through the hole in the wall."

"Did you find out who it was?" one of the listeners asked.

"Naw," said Uncle Billy. "I figured if anyone was that spunky, I'd just let him go. Besides, I didn't really want to know what kind of a guy would put his kid up to stealing anyway. But I did nail a bunch of boards over the hole, and the stealing stopped."

"I'll bet it was Slade's dad," Tracy whispered to Samantha.

"Tracy!" Samantha scolded.

"Well, they say he was born at the racetrack."

"Tracy, Slade's dad is only in his forties. He wasn't even born then."

"Well, then his grandfather. Those Langs have always been no good. My mother says so."

"Oh, Tracy, hush," Samantha said, wondering what Mrs. Wilson was telling her daughter about "those Kellys" these days.

Tracy's father came out of the kitchen just then, and she got one of those "I've been caught" looks on her face.

"Tracy!" She was in trouble now.

Samantha watched in disgust as her friend scampered over to her father and gave him her brightest smile. "Hi, Dad. I was just listening to one of Uncle Billy's stories." Her father glanced over at Samantha and hustled his daughter off toward the grandstand.

"Now, Samantha," Uncle Billy tried to soothe over her hurt feelings. "Just don't pay no attention to that Bert Wilson. He's ignorant just like the rest of those people who bought that story about your dad. How's your grandpa, by the way? Still pushing those Holsteins around."

"Yes," Samantha answered, glad that he had changed the subject. "Grandpa's doing real well. Grandma's driving a Beamer."

"No kidding?" said Uncle Billy. "Well, I remember when she was driving an old 1940 Ford pickup that they couldn't use at night because the lights ran the battery down. Those were the days. I always admired those two. They had spunk." He stood up to leave. "Oh, yeah. Is Cal Reed still leading and feeding 'em down south?"

"He is," Samantha replied, "but I think he's cutting down. He sold us a couple of his broodmares. Are you and Marcie still living on the ranch?"

"Yep. Got lots of fancy chickens." Uncle Billy also liked birds.

"And horses?" Samantha knew Uncle Billy always had at least one. Grandpa always said Billy Norton would never be able to get completely out of the horse business.

"Well, yes, one Appy colt. I don't even know why I bought him, but the guy who sold him to me really needed the money. Colt looks pretty good, though. I thought I'd ask your dad to train him next year. 'Course I'd rather sell him and let someone else fork out the day money."

Like Grandpa. Those old trainers never liked to own any horses.

"You want to go over to the stands for the last race?" Uncle Billy asked.

"I don't think so, but thanks," Samantha replied. "I'm not having a real good day." She didn't tell him that she was going back to the coach to find her uncle. She still had some real tough questions to ask him.

When she got home, she wasn't surprised that no one was there. She put a TV dinner in the microwave and popped a tape in the VCR. It was "Seabiscuit," and Samantha had heard stories about the filming from friends of hers who had been in the movie.

She tried to concentrate on the movie, but her mind kept wandering. She kept wondering where her father was and what he was doing. She reassured herself with the knowledge that he was somewhere nearby and that he was keeping an eye on her and her horse. He was also working on clearing his name. But who was the real culprit anyway? Slade's name popped into her head, but she didn't really think he was smart enough to pull off this kind of a scheme. *Uncle Jack? No way! He'd never hurt an animal, and he sure wouldn't get his brother-in-law into a mess like this. Then who?*

Chapter X

A STORM'S BREWING

A bright flash of lightning followed by a tremendous crack of thunder that shook the whole trailer awoke Samantha in the middle of the night. She glanced at the digital clock; it was dead. *Power's off,* she thought, just as another flash lit up the room. *Chug! He hates thunderstorms!*

Frantically, she scrambled into her jeans and jacket and rummaged in the closet for her rubber boots.

Downstairs, she could see that Uncle Jack had come in sometime during the night. He was snoring loudly. The thunder hadn't even caused him to roll over or blink an eye. She gave a quick sniff for any sign that he'd been drinking, but all she could smell was his aftershave and Juicy Fruit gum. *A cover-up? Nah...*

In the kitchen, she found the flashlight in the drawer where they always kept it and checked to make sure it worked. Then, she pulled the hood up on her jacket and ventured out into the stormy night.

The driving rain pelted her face, and without the streetlights, the backstretch was as dark as the inside of a Pharoah's tomb, but a whole lot wetter. Samantha had traveled the lanes at this fair so many times, however, she knew exactly where to go. She flashed the light back and forth in front of her feet as she sloshed along, missing most of the big puddles.

When she reached Barn C, she saw a faint light in their tack room and figured the thunder had awakened Joey also, but as she got closer, she heard voices arguing.

That's strange. But then, so was everything else these days.

When she looked in on Chug, the big colt was sleeping peacefully, stretched out on the straw like a baby. *Guess he has grown up after all.* She couldn't help remembering the little colt who had freaked during the occasional thunderstorm at home in Southern California.

She was about to return to her nice, warm bed when the voices in the tack room got louder. Samantha crept closer. Maybe her dad was there. Then she heard a familiar, always irritating, voice.

"Come on, Joey, have a little smoke." It was Slade, and he was trying to get their groom in trouble. As if they didn't have enough trouble already. *What a creep!*

"No way," came the reply. "I got a good job here, and I don't want to mess things up."

"Oh, you're not gonna lose your job from smokin' a little weed," Slade coaxed in a sickeningly sweet voice. "I'm your friend. I wouldn't do anything to get you in trouble."

"You're not my friend," Joey replied. "You don't have any friends. Besides, you do bad things to horses. I saw you over at Pinky's barn."

Samantha sucked in her breath in surprise when she heard that. She crept closer and peeked cautiously through the bottom corner of the window in the door of the tack room. Even in the dim light from a battery-operated lantern, she could see Slade's face cloud up as Joey spoke.

"You druggie moron," he threatened, dropping the marijuana on the floor in his anger. "You ever tell anybody you saw me at Pinky's, and I'll tell security I found that grass in your room. Then, I'll come back and bash out what's left of your brains."

"I never told anybody," Joey protested. "I don't want any trouble."

"That's right," Slade sneered. "Who'd believe you anyway? I'd just tell them you did it."

112

"Why don't you just go away and leave me alone," Joey complained, scratching his forehead nervously as he sat down on his cot.

"Just remember what I told you."

Slade turned to leave, and Samantha ducked noiselessly into Harlequin's empty stall. She flattened herself against the wall, hardly daring to breathe. The tack room door slammed, and she heard Slade carelessly sloshing away through the puddles.

The shed row lights came on suddenly just as Samantha felt something brush against her outstretched hand. She looked down to see a huge gray wolf spider right next to hand. *Oh my gosh!* Her usual composure crumbled. She was tougher than most girls about everything except spiders. She couldn't even watch the movie, "Arachnophobia."

She wanted to scream, but she was afraid that would bring Slade running back. Every muscle in her body was tense as she waited and watched the loathsome creature next to her hand. Her rational self told her it was only a wolf spider, not a black widow, and probably not dangerous. Her primitive self just wanted to scream and run.

Then, as quickly as it had appeared, it jumped off the wall into the straw and disappeared. Samantha let out a "whoosh" and her whole body slumped as she tried to slow down her racing heartbeat. She hated spiders more than anything.

Anxious to get out of the stall, she slipped over to the tack room and knocked gently on the door.

"Go away, Slade," Joey called from inside.

"Joey, it's me, Samantha," she said in a loud whisper. "Open up. I need to talk to you."

The door opened a crack. "Jeez, Samantha, can't it wait until morning?"

"Please, Joey, I heard what you and Slade were talking about."

Joey switched on the light and grudgingly opened the door. "What do you want, Samantha?" he demanded. He looked at his watch. "It's 3:30 in the morning."

Samantha pushed her way inside and closed the door. Joey sat down on the end of the bed, scratching his forehead. She noticed the marijuana cigarette still lying on the floor.

"I'm really proud of you for not smoking that joint," she said.

Joey brightened a little. "Really?"

"Definitely," she continued. "You really stood up to that sleazy Slade Lang."

Sleazy Slade Lang. Perfect!

"Anyhow," the girl went on, "did you really see Slade at Pinky's barn that night?"

Joey didn't say anything and just sat staring at the wall.

"Joey," she coaxed, "if you saw Slade, you have to tell. It will clear my dad."

He looked up at the girl. She could see he was extremely distressed. "I can't, Samantha." He ran his fingers nervously through his hair, scratching.

"Joey, my dad's been really good to you."

"I know, and I'm sorry, but you heard Slade say what he'd do to me if I ratted. I know he will too. I just know it. Besides, who'd believe me anyway?"

"I believe you, Joey."

He didn't answer. He just busied himself with sweeping the marijuana cigarette into a McDonald's napkin that had been on his nightstand. He folded the packet carefully and handed it to Samantha.

"Could you get rid of this for me? If anyone finds it here, I'm busted."

She put the packet carefully into her pocket and continued trying to persuade their groom. "Joey, listen. You've got to tell. Otherwise my dad will lose his license for good. He might even go to jail."

That's when it hit her. *He might even go to jail.* All along, she had been fooling herself into thinking it was just a matter of time before the whole mess was cleared up, but now, she saw the reality of the situation clearly. She had to convince Joey to come forward. There was no other way.

"If I tell, Slade will come after me," Joey said, but she had some hope that he was at least thinking it over.

"Please Joey." Pleading wasn't exactly her style, but she was desperate.

And then, he said something truly bizarre. "It isn't the fact that you're dead that counts, but only how did you die, right?"

It was a line from Edmund Vance Cook's poem about fighting the good fight and dying bravely if you had to. She knew it by heart. Joey was at least thinking about doing the right thing. With this tiny glimmer of hope, Samantha put on her most charming smile. "I didn't know you liked poetry, Joey."

Joey looked like he was trying to remember something. "Used to, I guess," he offered. "I remember my mom reading poetry to me when I was a little kid."

"Mine too!" Samantha exclaimed. Maybe she was making a little progress. Maybe she'd found a common ground. "My whole family loves poetry. See, we have a lot in common, don't you think?"

"I guess," came the reply.

"Then you'll help us?"

"No," Joey answered. He seemed more confused. "I don't want to talk about it anymore. Would you please leave? I have to get up in a couple of hours."

He started scratching his forehead again, and Samantha could tell he was becoming more agitated. She turned and opened the door. She could work on him some more tomorrow.

"Promise you'll just think about it, Joey," she said softly. "It means everything to us. When we get this mess cleared up, maybe we can read some poetry together."

"Charge of the Light Brigade?" Joey's face brightened a little. "It was always one of my favorites."

"Absolutely! It's one of my favorites too," the girl said, making a mental note to dig out the worn *Family Book of Favorite Poems* as soon as she got home.

Outside, she bent her arm like she was pulling a slot machine."Cha-ching!" They had the culprit and her dad would soon be in the clear and back to work. Chug would run in the futurity for sure.

The rain had stopped, and a gazillion stars were smiling down at her. The air smelled clean and fresh after the rain, and she could hear the night sounds of crickets and frogs again. She looked up, put her hands together and said, "Thank you."

Chapter XI

WHO'S IN TROUBLE NOW?

When Samantha awoke early the next morning, the little bird was back in the tree singing, "Cheer-up, cheerily,"

"I will, cheerily," she sang back as she dressed. It was a beautiful morning that forecast another beautiful day. *Beautiful in more ways than one...*

Uncle Jack was still asleep, but she gently shook him. She had to tell him about last night. "Come on, Uncle Jack, please wake up."

"Go away, Sam," he protested, pulling the covers over his head.

"No, Uncle Jack," the girl persisted. "I know who drugged Pinky's horse."

Uncle Jack sat straight up like he'd been shot. "What?" He rubbed the sleep out of his eyes.

"It was Slade Lang," she blurted out. "Joey saw him."

"Why that little S.O.B. -- oh, sorry, Sam." He was wide-awake now. "So, we've got a witness? Put the coffee on while I shower," he directed.

Samantha went into the kitchen and fixed her uncle some coffee and made a hot chocolate for herself. She thought about making some breakfast, but she was too excited to eat.

Cups in hand, Uncle Jack and his niece hurried over to the barn. She filled him in on the details. When they arrived, however, their hopes were dashed in an instant. Joey was gone -- tote bag, family photo and all!

"He bailed," Samantha choked, blinking back tears of disappointment and anger. "Slade's threats worked, after all. Let's go get that creep."

"Now, hold on, girl," her uncle cautioned. "We can't just go accusing him without a witness or some kind of proof."

"I'll beat it out of him," Samantha retorted, flexing the muscles in her right arm and making a fist. "He's a coward; he'll fold."

"Samantha, get hold of yourself," her uncle counseled. "We've got to find a better way."

"Then, let's haul him up in front of the stewards," she suggested, desperate for justice. "He'll crack under pressure."

"Do you really think so?"

"Not, really," Samantha admitted. "But we've got to do something, Uncle Jack. This time, he's gone too far. He's ruined my dad's reputation, and besides, he might do something to another horse if he isn't stopped. He might do something to Chug."

That was a terrifying thought, and she turned and ran down to Chug's stall to see if he was okay. Chug was fine. He greeted her with a whinny between mouthfuls of hay. At least Joey had fed the horse before he left.

"Now," said Uncle Jack, coming up behind his niece and draping an affectionate arm around her shoulder. "Let's put our heads together and come up with a plan. We're Kellys and Malones – nobody gets the best of us."

*   *   *

Two hours later, when they knew most of the horsemen would be at home getting ready for the races, Samantha called Jeff. Her fingers were trembling as she punched the tiny buttons on her uncle's cell phone. She hoped she could sound convincing and pull this off. They were desperate.

"Hey, Jeff," she said when her friend answered, hoping her big, fake smile would carry over in her voice.

"Hey, Sam. What's up?"

"Well," she said, trying to sound casual. "I watched Warhawk work this morning. *That part was true, at least. She had watched the colt briefly.* I think we ought to work them together and see how they do."

"Great idea!" Jeff was enthusiastic. "How about Saturday?"

"Super!" Samantha exclaimed. She really did think it would be fun to see them run together.

"I'll talk to my dad and set it up."

"Oh, and Jeff," she went on. *This is the hard part.* "I want to make peace with Slade. *Not.* I've got too many problems in my life right now to keep the feud going."

"Are you serious!" Jeff sounded amazed.

Oh boy. He's on to me now.

"Dead straight," Samantha said with what she hoped was conviction. "We might have to ask your dad to train Chug if my dad doesn't get cleared in time for the Cal-Bred. I don't want to be fighting with Slade if we do. In fact, why don't you guys come over for lunch? I've got sloppy Joes, and Ida Mae brownies." *I feel like such a worm, lying to Jeff like this.*

Jeff hesitated. "Well, I'll be there, but I can't promise about my brother."

"Give it a try," Samantha insisted cheerfully. *Mom always says, "Nothing beats a try but a*

121

failure." Clicking the "off" button on the phone, she pulled some hamburger out of the fridge and started browning it in a large pan.

Uncle Jack grabbed his hat and turned to leave. "Keep your chin up. I'll be close by."

*   *   *

Half an hour later, she saw the two Lang brothers coming toward the coach. She was surprised to see that, this time, they didn't look all that different. Slade had on a clean Western shirt, Levis with no holes, and his hair was neatly combed. Her conscience was trying to get the best of her when she quickly reminded herself of the sleezy Slade she had heard last night.

"Come on in, guys," she said in her most charming voice. "Lunch's almost ready."

Jeff stepped inside; Slade tripped on the doorstep.

He's nervous. She was amazed. She'd never seen Slade rattled by anything but his father before today. *Good.*

Jeff slid into the dinette seat by the open kitchen window, followed by his brother.

"Before we eat, let's talk a little," Samantha said. She sat down across from them.

"Sure, Sam," Jeff said with his easy smile." What do you want to talk about?"

122

She dropped the bomb.

"I just wanted to ask Slade where he thinks Joey might have gone." She tried to remain casual, but her heart was beating wildly. She dug her fingernails into the palm of her hand to quiet her nerves. It was an old trick, but it usually worked. She hoped her face wasn't getting red; it sure felt hot.

"How should I know?" Slade said warily. "I don't hang around with that brain-fried druggie."

"You hung around with him last night," she ventured. " I heard you two arguing when I went down to the barn to check on my horse."

"Oh, that." Slade was still pretty cool. "Well, I hate to tell you this, Sammy, but he wanted me to get him some weed."

"Liar!" Samantha couldn't hold it back another minute. She just silently prayed that she wouldn't start crying like she sometimes did when she was hopping mad. "He wasn't asking you for drugs. You were trying to get him to take some. Then, he told you he saw you at Pinky's barn the night the horse was drugged, and you threatened to bash his brains out if he told anyone. Now he's gone."

Slade's face was had turned slightly redder, but he seemed relieved to hear that the only witness to the crime was gone.

"You offered him marijuana," she accused, "knowing he'd lose his job if he got caught with drugs."

The cool Slade began to take over. "Prove it," he challenged calmly. Jeff just sat there wide-eyed and tongue-tied.

Samantha took the folded paper napkin out of her pocket and laid it on the table. "I'll bet your fingerprints are all over this," she bluffed as she opened the packet exposing the illegal marijuana cigarette.

Slade snatched the packet off the table and stood up. "Now prove it," he said with a smug smile as he pocketed the marijuana.

All at once, Jeff found his voice. "You jerk. Did you really think you could get away with this?"

"I did get away with it," Slade said with a triumphant smile. "And Samantha's father's gonna pay for it. It was so easy, too. I watched this trailer for a week at Stockton until one day when Frank left his keys on the table while he was in the shower. Then I just sneaked in the door and lifted them."

Jeff was fuming. Samantha could see his fists clenched. His eyes were blazing.

"Then it was just a matter of finding a jug with your dad's fingerprints on it while that nitwit groom was over at the fair. The ultimate revenge for that little Easter Bunny incident, don't you think, Sammy?" he bragged.

Jeff sprang from his seat and lunged toward his brother. "I'll kill you for this, Slade!" he shouted.

"That'll do, son," came an authoritative voice, as the screen door opened suddenly. Samantha saw the old cowboy grab Slade from behind. Jeff backed off.

When she saw the man straight and tall, she suddenly realized who really had been shadowing her every move since she'd arrived.

"Dad!" Samantha was overjoyed. "You sure had me fooled!"

Frank Kelly pulled the struggling Slade over to the side of the door to let in Uncle Jack; his friend, Perry Miek who was a CHRB steward; and the track security officer, Del Hall.

"We heard it all through the kitchen window," Miek said with a sad shake of his head. Del Hall handcuffed Slade and sat him down at the table, but Slade wasn't finished yet.

"So what?" he argued. "It's all hearsay. You don't have any witnesses."

"I'm here," said Joey as he stepped into the already-crowded room. He stayed way back from Slade, but Samantha's smile of welcome was shyly returned. Uncle Jack called Jake Lang on his cell phone. Slade's father came puffing up a few minutes later.

"What's going on here?" he demanded.

"Well, Jake," Frank Kelly said sadly. "I'm afraid Slade, here, is in a lot of trouble."

"He drugged Pinky's horse, Dad," Jeff blurted out before anyone else had a chance to speak.

Samantha huddled close to her father, expecting a violent reaction from the boy's father, but Jake just shook his head and said quietly, "Is that true son?"

Slade looked contrite. He blinked back tears as he spoke. "I just wanted to make sure Warhawk won the Cal-Bred."

"Aw, son," Jake choked. He looked ashamed and heartbroken. "That's not the way to do it." The Langs, the steward and the security officer left the trailer together. Jeff was too embarrassed to look at anyone. Samantha wanted to go to him and tell him she knew he didn't have anything to do with it, but the group departed so quickly, she didn't have a chance.

"I knew he'd done it," Frank Kelly said. "I just couldn't prove it until Joey found me this morning and said he was willing to testify." He turned to his groom. "I'm real proud of you, son." Joey smiled bashfully.

"I almost didn't recognize you, sir," he said. Then added with a grin, "but I'd know those boots anywhere." Embarrassed by all the fuss, he excused himself to go and check on Chug. Samantha was embarrassed to think she hadn't recognized her father's boots too, but she hadn't really been that close to "the old cowboy."

"What's going to happen to Slade, Dad?" she asked.

"Well, he'll likely spend a little time in juvenile hall, I expect, seeing as he's not quite 18."

"It's about time," Uncle Jack put in. "This isn't the first thing that's happened at the track that had Slade's name written all over it."

"Well," Samantha hesitated, unsure how to broach the subject. Then she blurted out, "Since we're clearing up a lot of things, could you please tell me what it is that you *did* for those casino men from Reno."

"Bob and Charlie?" Uncle Jack seemed a little embarrassed. "How'd you know about that?"

"Well, the night you came home singing Danny Boy..."

"Oh, sorry, Sam," he groaned. "I guess I did tie a pretty good one on that night, but I haven't touched a drop since."

Frank Kelly looked sharply at his brother-in-law. "Let's have it, Jack."

"Well, I was going to tell you as soon as you got back," Uncle Jack explained. "I ran up a bit of a gambling debt when I was over in Reno. They wanted their money, but what they really wanted was for me to come back and tend bar over the winter. Even made me sign a contract."

Samantha's father let out a huge laugh. "Your chickens always come home to roost, don't they, Jack?"

Uncle Jack's good nature took over, and he laughed too. "Well, what can I say?" He threw up his hands in mock dismay. "They love me over there. I'm the best darned bartender they've ever had."

Samantha leaned close to her father. "I'm so glad you're back, Dad," she said with a happy grin. Frank put his arm around her and gave her a hug. "But, could you lose the beard and take a bath? You don't smell any too good."

"All part of the disguise," Frank answered with a grin, "You have to admit it had everyone fooled. I even had Uncle Billy scratching his head and thinking, 'I know this guy from somewhere, but I just can't seem to remember where."

"Good thing Joey recognized your boots," said Samantha, "or he might not have shown up today. It took me awhile just to convince him I was your daughter."

"Have to admit that took a bit of doing," Frank admitted. "He caught me in Chug's stall this morning and almost called security. Then I took him over to Tommy and Ida Rae's, and we called Jack and hatched up his little plan."

Samantha glanced over at her uncle. "You knew all along?"

"Sorry, Sweetheart," Jack said. "We couldn't tell you everything because we wanted to make sure your act was convincing. I told your dad that you and I had everything else planned, but having Joey here just put the icing on the cake."

*　　*　　*

That night, Jeff called and asked Samantha to meet him at the midway. They sat down in the little park to talk.

"You mad at me?" he ventured cautiously. She shook her head.

"You mad at me?" she asked shyly. "I got your brother into some major trouble."

"He got himself in trouble. I hope you don't think all the Langs are like that, Samantha."

"Not you, Jeff." She replied.

"Not my dad either," Jeff said firmly. "He's a grouch and mean sometimes because he still misses my mother, but he's an honest man, and he truly loves horses."

"I know," the girl answered.

"No, really, Sam," Jeff insisted. "He's so broken up about this, he keeps going around saying, 'Where did I go wrong?'"

"What do you think they'll do to your brother?"

"Well," Jeff brightened up a bit. "He'll probably get probation since it's his first offense. Then, Dad'll pack him off to the Colonel's."

"The Colonel's?"

"My mom's father. He's retired Marine Corps. Semper Fi, and all that. He'll whip Slade into shape. You'll see. I know because I've spent all my Christmas vacations with the Colonel and Aunt Christine ever since my mother died."

So that's why he's so different from his brother.

"By the way," Jeff changed the subject. "How about that twin workout on Saturday? Still on?"

"You bet." She held up her right hand, fingers outstretched for the high-five.

"Deal," Jeff said, slapping her hand gently and then closing his fingers around hers. "Want to go for a Ferris wheel ride?"

"Okay," Samantha replied, not knowing what else to say. Jeff had always been her best buddy, but now, all of a sudden, she was having some very different feelings about him. Maybe now that the trouble was over, she did have time to think about boys.

*　　*　　*

They rode the big wheel to the top, and with the noise and lights of the midway far below, it was like they were in a private world all their own. When the wheel jerked to a stop to take on passengers down below, Samantha grabbed Jeff's arm for safety. And that's when it happened. He slipped his arm around the girl and kissed her in the warm summer night just as the wheel started up again. The bottom dropped out of her stomach, and she couldn't tell if it was from the kiss or the ride, but she didn't care. One thing she knew for sure. The kiss was definitely not a "best buddy" kind of a kiss at all!

Chapter XII

TRIALS AND TRIBULATIONS

Samantha was sitting at the laptop in the kitchen working on a poem, when her friend, Tracy, knocked at the door. The fair circuit folk had moved from Pleasanton to Vallejo to Santa Rosa, and finally landed here at the Bay Meadows track in San Mateo. She and Jeff had been keeping steady company, but since Santa Rosa, she hadn't seen Tracy at all.

"Hey, Trace, come on in!" she said with a bright smile.

Her friend entered the Kelly coach and made herself comfortable at the table across from Samantha.

"I wasn't sure you guys were coming," Samantha said, pressing the print button on the computer.

"Miss coming to Bay Meadows? Are you kidding?" Tracy answered with a laugh. "My mom wouldn't miss this meet for anything in the world. She gets to rub elbows with all the big shot Thoroughbred trainers and go out to lunch with their wives. It's really her thing."

"Whatever," Samantha replied quietly.

"Sam, you're not still mad at her, are you?"

"Oh, I guess not, Trace. I'm just glad you're more like your father."

"Me too," Tracy admitted. "I'm not into the show horse thing at all. I couldn't tell the difference between a jumper and a dressage horse." Then she added, "But I could tell you about a seven-furlong claiming race for non-winners of two."

"Oh, yeah?" Samantha asked. "Well, other than a flower, what's a morning glory?"

"A horse who works like lightning in the morning and won't do diddley in the afternoon."

"Excellent. And a bug boy?"

"Easy," said Tracy. "That's an apprentice jockey."

"Right on," said Samantha. "You get an "A" in Horse Racing One."

"What were you working on when I came in," Tracy asked, noticing the paper in the printer.

"New poem," Samantha replied. "Want to read it?"

"Absolutely!" Tracy exclaimed. "You know, Sam, I never used to like poetry, but the stuff you write is about things I know and understand." She took the paper from her friend and started to read.

> *The Appaloosa*
> *He's half a ton of strength and energy,*
> *But he responds to my small hand.*
> *He's fifteen and a half hands high,*
> *But he's careful of my feet.*
>
> *He gets cold and tired and hungry,*
> *But he's always cheerful when I bring him food.*
>
> *He's a winner at the track,*
> *Can run the oval with the best,*
> *But he's never snooty about it.*
>
> *He's got a history as old as time itself.*
> *Kings and lords rode his ancestors to battle,*
> *But his pals are a shaggy pony and a ragtail mutt.*
>
> *He was here before me, hunting buffalo and deer, and*
> *His forefathers carried the Nez Perce into battle with*
> *mine,*
> *But he'll show me his hills and valleys,*
> *And take me to the icy stream where he played as a colt.*
>
> *He could have raced away,*
> *And remained afar in the lush green pasture,*
> *But when I came to see the babies, he picked me.*
> *And now, that big, beautiful, spotted Appaloosa*
> *Is my very best friend.*

"It's awesome," Tracy said quietly.

"Well, I took a little poetic license with where he was born," Samantha explained, "but who wants to read about a little crippled colt anyway?"

"They might if he turned out to be Sierra Warrior," Tracy said gleefully. She was almost as enthusiastic about Chug as Samantha was.

"Speaking of which," Samantha said, looking at her watch. "It's time to go over to the track. We've got the first three races today. Think your mom would have a problem with you watching Appaloosas, Trace?"

"That's mean," Tracy pouted.

"Just kidding," said Samantha with a bright smile. "Let's go have some fun."

For all her seemingly light-heartedness, Samantha was a bundle of nerves inside. The first three races today were actually the trials to determine which horses would run in the Cal-Bred Futurity next week. There were only ten slots on the futurity card, and some thirty horses had been entered. Only the fastest ten would make it to the finals.

Chug was in the first race, Warhawk the second, and Pinky's horse, War Eagle II, who had recovered nicely after his near-death experience, was running in the third. *Near death experience?* All at once, she got this bizarre mental picture of Pinky's horse trotting along through a long dark tunnel with a

135

bright white light at the end. She was about to laugh when she remembered Galadriel. That thought of the filly's tragic death sobered her up in an instant and brought her back to the present.

The two girls arrived at the saddling paddock just as Frank Kelly was putting the small racing saddle on Chug. "Speaking of bug boys," said Tracy. "Look who's riding your horse."

"Stevie Johnson?" Samantha was alarmed. "Where's Pat?"

She flashed her I.D. and went through the gate into the saddling area.

Arriving at the number three stall, she asked, "Dad, where's Pat?"

"Stuck in traffic," her father answered, tapping the cell phone at his waist. "There's a big wreck out on Highway 101, and he won't be here until at least the fifth race. Lucky for us, Stevie was here." He indicated the young man standing next to him.

"Hi Samantha," the jockey offered with a shy smile.

"Hi Steve," Samantha returned politely, trying not to let on how disappointed she was.

Pat Carillo had always been their jockey of choice. He had a string of winners a mile long and years of experience. In contrast, Stevie had only been riding since this year. He had promise they all said, but Samantha was worried. This was a big race. *Oh, well. With an apprentice jockey, Chug will carry less weight. That's a little consolation. He'll get out of the gate a little faster, and that may give him a slight edge.*

She heard her dad talking to the jockey. "Now, Steve, remember, this is only a trial. We probably only need to run at least third to get into the final race. No need to kill the horse or yourself. We don't have to break any records today."

"I can do this, Mr. Kelly," the young man said confidently.

Confident, not cocky. Samantha liked that.

"Riders up," called the paddock judge. Frank gave Stevie a leg up, and handed the horse off to Wilma as they started for the post parade.

When Samantha looked up at her father wondering why he wasn't ponying Chug, he explained, "I want to watch this one from the stands, Sam."

Chug had won one race at Santa Rosa and come in second in another, but this race was the best running against the best. Samantha was disappointed that Stevie was riding instead of Pat, but, like her father had said, they only had to finish third.

Tracy joined them, and as the three of them walked over to the track, Samantha was remembering the win at Santa Rosa. It was he most exciting day she'd ever had. Chug's first race, and he had won easily. She'd gotten so excited, she'd spilled a whole strawberry drink down the front of her clothes. So, instead of glamorous Samantha Kelly, owner, in the winner's circle graciously acknowledging accolades from her friends and family, she'd been sloppy Sam, hiding behind the horse's hindquarters for the win picture. A month later, it was pretty funny to think about, but at the time she'd been mortified.

"The horses have reached the gate," the announcer called. "Number one is in. There goes number two."

Samantha watched the big screen. Chug was balking a little. She held her breath, powerless to do anything from so far away.

"Easy, Stevie," her father directed under his breath, and then Chug was in the gate.

The bell rang. "And they're running! Sierra Warrior takes the early lead, with Apache Princess and Minidoka Minnie right behind. Streak O' Lightning is in fourth, followed by Arkansas Traveler and Crazy Mary. Indian Schoolgirl and Easy Go Lightly trail the field."

Samantha felt Jeff come up and slip his arm around her, but she didn't want to take her eyes off the race. She said, "Hi," without turning.

"And it's Sierra Warrior around the turn. Apache Princess is in second a length ahead of the rest of the field.

"Sierra Warrior is still leading, with Apache Princess in second and a gap of two to Minidoka Minnie, running third. And here comes Streak O' Lightning on the outside.

"And down the stretch they come! It's Sierra Warrior opening up a half-length lead. Apache Princess and Streak O' Lightning are battling for second, and Minidoka Minnie has the rail in fourth.

"Sierra Warrior by half a length, with Streak O' Lightning and Apache Princess. Minidoka Minnie is looking for racing room as they near the wire."

As the horses flashed past the finish line, Samantha turned and gave Jeff a big hug. "We did it! Wire to wire! Come on, Jeff!"

"Group hug!" said Tracy, including herself in, and the Three Musketeers raced off for the winner's circle.

Stevie was grinning from ear to ear as he steered the colt into the ring. Frank Kelly said, "Nice ride," and reached for Chug's bridle. Samantha gave her horse a big hug and stood proudly in front of him as the photographer snapped the picture.

"Well, I hope Warhawk does something in his race," Jeff said as they walked back to the grandstand. "I'll see you later, Sam. I've got to help Dad saddle since Slade's not here."

"I'll wait for you here," the girl answered.

"Excuse me, Miss Kelly," said a young woman, tapping Samantha gently on the shoulder. "I'm Joy Carroll from *The Appaloosa Journal*. Can we talk for a minute?"

Miss Kelly? The Appaloosa Journal?

Tracy's eyes were as big as saucers as she nudged her friend in the ribs. Samantha hesitated briefly and then said, "Sure."

"Well, I'm doing a story on the Cal-Bred," the young woman explained, "and I'd just like to get your feelings about your horse winning his futurity trial and what his chances are in the final race."

"He's gonna win, of course," Tracy offered. "Chug's the best!"

"Chug?" the reporter questioned.

"Well," Samantha began. "We called him Chugalug when he was a baby because he was such a greedy little guy." She went on to tell about how Chug had been born and how they'd had to bottle-feed him for a month until he was strong enough to nurse.

"Wow! This is great," said the reporter. "Mind if I use it in my article? Sort of a Cinderella story, don't you think? Hard start in life and then comes back to win his heat of the Cal-Bred Futurity Trials."

"And then wins the big race," Tracy piped up.

"Wouldn't that be a wonderful ending," said the journalist enthusiastically. "I got a shot of

Sierra Warrior in the winner's circle, but could we take one of you and your horse back at the barn or something?"

"Come on," said Samantha, beginning to get into the swing of being interviewed and enjoying the idea of Chug's being featured in the national Appaloosa publication. "They should be done at the test barn by now."

When they were back at the Kelly barn, the reporter took several pictures of Samantha cooling out the horse. And then she got the picture she was looking for as Samantha took Chug's head between her hands and planted a great big kiss on his nose.

"Perfect!" the reporter exclaimed. "Maybe we'll even make the cover." Samantha smiled shyly, and Tracy shouted, "Yes!"

*　　　*　　　*

At the end of the day, all of Samantha's favorites had qualified for the Cal-Bred Futurity. Warhawk had run second and Pinky's horse; War Eagle II, had won his trial. Best of all, they had all finished sound and would be ready for the big race next week.

Chapter XIII

THE BIG DAY

On the morning of the Cal-Bred Futurity at Bay Meadows Race Track in San Mateo, the Kelly coach was filled to overflowing. Gram was frying bacon, Ann Kelly was making pancakes, and Samantha was setting up dishes for a buffet breakfast. They'd have to eat outside because there wasn't room in the little dinette for all of the clan.

Frank and his father already had their coffee, and they were outside at the picnic table talking race talk with Uncle Billy Norton. As she placed the plates on the table, Samantha was smiling and humming which caused her mother and grandmother to exchange knowing looks. Chug wasn't the only reason the girl was happy these days.

After breakfast, Samantha and her father took Grandpa and Uncle Billy Norton down to the barns to see Chug. They found War Eagle's owner, Cliff Elliott, already admiring this son of his stallion.

Gramps shook hands with his old friend and asked, "You bring Cal along?"

"No way," Cliff laughed. "You couldn't pry Cal Reed off that ranch with a stick. He's always 'waitin' for a horse to come in.'"

They all laughed because they knew it was true. For Samantha, Cal's always being at the ranch had been a real boon. She used his extensive library of horse books for research. He had also patiently answered all of her questions and offered advice, not just on her term papers, but on training Chug as well. She really wished Cal were here, though, because, in a way, he had gotten it all started. His "Sierra" bloodlines were all over the pedigrees of many of the horses in the race.

"Well, I've looked over all the entries," said Elliott seriously. "It's a tough field."

"So who do you like?" Samantha asked, just knowing it would have to be Chug.

"Well, your colt's nice, and so is his half-brother," Elliott answered, thoughtfully stroking his gray beard. "Pinky's colt looks good too. Came off that lay-up real well."

Samantha knew War Eagle II was now a contender. He'd come back well enough to win his futurity trial last week.

"He's kin too, you know," Elliott continued. "He's out of a full-sister to Eagle."

"No kidding? I didn't know that," said Grandpa. He had once told Samantha that all Thoroughbreds could trace their ancestry back to three great stallions, the Godolphin Arabian, the Darley Arabian and the Beyerly Turk. You could find a common ancestor somewhere in every pedigree. It was getting to be the same with Appaloosas. If one horse sired a lot of winners, breeders would take their mares to him.

Grandpa also said that at almost any time, anywhere, most horsemen could find a mutual friend in the horse world. Grandpa said you could go clear to Australia and meet up with another horseman, and within twenty minutes, you would come up with a horse or a horseman you both knew. The horse business was just one big family. Samantha, herself, had found out how true it was a couple of years ago.

She and her grandparents were on vacation, heading for Texas, when Grandpa spotted a sign advertising the Rex Allen Museum in Wilcox, Arizona. They had stopped in the tiny town that was off I-10 out in the middle of the big nowhere between Tucson and El Paso. A big fan of Western movies, Grandpa wanted to see the place that honored one of his favorite old-time movie stars.

The museum was in a storefront, and it was as tiny as the town, but very nice. There were cases displaying Rex Allen's beautiful fancy Western costumes and pictures everywhere. Samantha was admiring an especially pretty satin shirt decorated with embroidered roses when she heard Grandpa exclaim, "Well, I'll be! Look, Sam. It's Cal."

And there he was! In the picture Cal was standing next to a big leopard Appaloosa horse, grinning in his familiar, quirky way. Samantha had called Cal that night and asked him if he'd known that he was famous enough to be in a museum.

"Well, I know I'm old enough to be in a museum," he had chuckled.

Suddenly, Samantha looked down at her watch. She'd have to go right now if she wanted a turn in the shower.

Back at the coach, Samantha's mother had a surprise for her – a new teal green and white striped Western shirt and a pair of matching Wranglers.

"Gee thanks, Mom," the girl said with a grin. New dresses didn't particularly light her up, but new jeans were a whole different story.

"Well, I thought you might want to dress up a little for the race. Look inside the pocket. I found the perfect earrings."

"I'll polish your boots for a dollar," James piped up. He was playing Minesweeper on the laptop.

145

"For a dollar, I'll do it myself, you little con man," she laughed. She noticed that her brother was freshly scrubbed and was also wearing new clothes. His wet hair was neatly combed, and even his fingernails looked clean for a change. When she looked at her own broken nails, she hoped there'd be time enough for a quick manicure before the race.

After showering and getting dressed, Samantha padded her way into the kitchen in her stocking feet. "Gram, would you French braid my hair? You're so good at it."

Her grandmother fluffed the girl's long, naturally curly hair and said, "It's not hot today, Sweetheart. There's a nice breeze blowing in from the bay. Why don't you just wear your hair down?"

"That nice breeze would turn it into a big frizzy mess in five minutes," Samantha protested.

"Well, tie it in back then," her grandmother suggested. "You have such pretty hair. You should let people see it once in awhile."

"Well, okay," the girl agreed. There was one person she might like to see it.

"And Sam," her mother added. "Put some makeup on for a change, and look like a girl."

*   *   *

Half an hour before the race, Cliff Elliott's "War Eagle" box seats were filled to overflowing. Samantha and James sat with their mother and grandparents, and Uncle Jack was in the next row with the Elliotts and Uncle Billy Norton. Pinky Mason's parents and Jeff's grandparents, the Colonel and Mrs. Lumsden, were seated behind them. They were in town to pick up Slade, who had to spend a week in juvenile hall before he would be released to them.

Samantha had wanted to escort Chug to the saddling paddock for the big race, but Joey had looked so disappointed at the suggestion, she had backed off and let him do it. She figured he'd earned the honor.

Much to Samantha's embarrassment, James had insisted on wearing the big, foam rubber cowboy hat she had bought him. "Mom," she complained. "He looks like a geek."

"Leave him alone, Samantha," her mother had said gently. James had grinned and stuck out his tongue at her.

She heard the call to post and beamed with pride as her father led Sierra Warrior out onto the track for the post parade. Frank Kelly looked tall and strong riding his Appaloosa pony horse, and when she glanced at her mother, she could see that Ann Kelly was still very much in love with her trainer husband. Her eyes had kind of a dreamy look, and she was smiling broadly.

Joey had groomed Chug until his coat glistened so bright in the sunlight of the beautiful California afternoon, it almost hurt Samantha's eyes just to look at him. Wearing the Kelly colors of white with green shamrocks, Pat Carillo completed what Samantha thought was a truly spectacular picture. She knew she would remember this day forever.

The colt walked calmly beside the pony, and Samantha had a hard time equating this magnificent creature with the little colt that they had almost put to sleep. Today he *was* Sierra Warrior!

The number two horse was Warhawk, almost a mirror image of his half-brother except for a sock on his left hind leg. He was also calm as Jake Lang led him in front of the grandstand. Wilma was ponying Pinky's horse, War Eagle II, the bells on her tack jingling as she led the horse in front of the stands.

Each horse wore a blue saddle cloth monogrammed in white with his post position number and the words "Cal-Bred Futurity." *They are really spectacular. I just love the Appaloosas because they're all so different. Well, usually.* She laughed to herself. She still had trouble telling Chug and Warhawk apart, and one of them was her very own horse!

Apache Princess was fourth, and as she passed the stands, everyone agreed that she was flat gorgeous. Grandpa always said there was nothing prettier than a two-year-old filly, and Princess proved him right. She was all black, with just a sprinkling of white snowflakes over her hindquarters. Samantha loved the delicate, feminine arch of her neck and her delightfully dainty head. She was as graceful as a gazelle. The breeze fluffed her silky mane and tail as she pranced in front of the stands, and Samantha could see they were tipped with silver. Princess wasn't finished changing color yet. It would be fun to see her next year.

That was the neat thing about Appaloosas. You never knew what you were going to get when the babies were born. You just hoped for color, any color. Then, some of them changed completely when they matured. One of Ann's old mares had turned completely white over the years with only her beautiful human-like eyes and her striped hooves to tell you she was an Appaloosa. Funny thing was, if you wet her down, you could still see her spotted skin under the white coat.

When the last horses passed the stands, Samantha started to fidget. She read her program for the gazillionth time, she looked across the infield at the starting gate, and she watched the horses on the big screen. She just couldn't sit still. Finally, she excused herself and ran down to watch the race from the rail. Jeff found her there, right in front of the finish line standing next to Ida Mae.

"Well, Doll Baby," said the older woman to the girl, "I've got twenty bucks on Chuggy. I hope he does it, 'cause I need some more yarn."

Samantha laughed. Ida Mae had a whole cabinet in her trailer just stuffed full of yarn.

"Hey, Sam," Jeff said from behind them. As she turned to greet him, she noticed that he, too, was wearing new clothes and they looked good on him. Unconsciously, she tucked a loose strand of hair back and tossed her head slightly, the little silver horse earrings dancing in the sunlight.

"You look – uh – great, Samantha," he said shyly.

"You don't look half bad yourself," she answered, trying to act nonchalant. She noticed that he was carrying a small package wrapped in brown paper. "What's that?"

"Later," he said as he slipped an arm easily around her waist. "You smell good too." Samantha leaned against him and giggled. She had always hated it when Tracy giggled, but somehow now, when Jeff was around, she found she just couldn't help herself. And, he'd been around a lot in the last few weeks.

"Listen, Sam," Jeff said seriously. "No matter who wins, let's both get in the win picture. Okay?"

"Deal."

"The horses are at the gate," came the announcement. Samantha turned when she heard the bell, trying to pick Chug out of the runners on the other side of the track.

"And they're running! War Eagle II takes the early lead with Sierra Warrior in second and Warhawk running third. Apache Princess is fourth and Streak O' Lightning is fifth, followed by Arkansas Traveler, Minidoka Minnie, and Indian Schoolgirl. Crazy Mary and Easy Go Lightly trail the field as they round the first turn."

"Come on, Chug!" Samantha screamed. Jeff looked down at her and smiled.

"Come on, Warhawk!" he shouted louder. She glanced quickly up at him, and they both laughed. Tracy pushed her way in between Ida Mae and Samantha.

"Sorry I'm late," she said, trying to catch her breath. "I wouldn't have missed this for the world!"

"Now it's Sierra Warrior on the outside challenging War Eagle II for the lead. Warhawk is third looking for racing room on the rail. Apache Princess and Streak O' Lightning are right there."

"Keep after him, Jorge!" she heard Pinky Mason yell from down the rail.

"As the field turns for home, it's War Eagle II still in the lead, Warhawk second and Sierra Warrior third.

"Down the stretch they come! War Eagle II is the leader with Warhawk and Sierra Warrior battling for second, a length ahead of Apache Princess."

"Push him, push him," Jake Lang shouted to his jockey.

The horses blazed by the grandstand, and in less than a minute, it was all over. "And it's War Eagle II to win by a neck!" shouted the announcer. "What a finish!"

Pinky was running and jumping and whooping. As he passed the three young people, he grabbed their arms. "Come on, Shorty. I want all my friends in the winner's circle. Ida Mae, bring Tommy too!"

Samantha was disappointed in Chug, but Pinky's enthusiasm, was so contagious, she just couldn't stay sad.

Oh, what the heck? She thought. Pink deserves it anyway. Glancing at the scoreboard, she saw that Warhawk had finished second, and Chug was a respectable third. They'd each get a good paycheck.

By the time War Eagle II returned to the winner's circle, the ring was filled with Masons, Kellys, Langs and Elliotts. Everyone was laughing and crying and congratulating. They draped a beautiful blue and yellow Cal-Bred Futurity blanket over the horse, and Pinky was about to burst with pride. This time, his tears were happy ones. They all shouted, "Cheers!" and the photographer snapped the picture. Cliff Elliott ordered 20 copies.

Then, Samantha felt Jeff tugging at her elbow. "Come on." He pulled her through the gate, past the betting windows under the grandstand and out onto the fairgrounds. She was totally mystified.

"Jeff, where are we going?"

"Just come on," he insisted, guiding her through the crowd.

He stopped in a somewhat secluded garden area, and Samantha flopped down on a wrought-iron bench to catch her breath and collect her wits.

For a moment, she was lost in thought, and then she said,"I'm glad Pinky won."

"Me too," Jeff admitted. "After what my brother did, Pinky deserved some good luck."

"But I have to admit I'm disappointed. I was just so sure Chug would win."

"Samantha, he had only been out a few times before the trials. War Eagle and Warhawk had a lot more experience. I think he did great. Besides, before the season's over, Chug will beat Warhawk, and Warhawk will beat War Eagle. They'll just keep trading wins until it's time to go home for the winter.

Like they say, on any given day, the best horse *that day* wins."

"And think about next year when they're three-year-olds," Samantha brightened. Her eyes took on a dreamy expression. "Won't the Cal-Bred Derby be something else?"

"That's my girl," Jeff said. Then, without a word, he offered her the small package he had been carrying throughout the race.

She glanced up at the boy, and then slid a neatly manicured fingernail under the tape that held the wrapping. Inside, she found a little heart-shaped wooden plaque with a black and white Appaloosa horse painted on it. She looked up at Jeff, her eyes sparkling. "It's beautiful."

Carefully, she read the verse that was printed beneath the little horse:

Roses are red, violets are blue,
I'm not much at rhyming, but I do love you!
Jeff

Samantha was charmed. She held the little plaque close to her heart. "I love it!" she said with a sweet smile. All in all, it had turned out to be the very best summer of her entire life!

End

About The Author

Nancy Sanderson grew up in the suburbs of Chicago reading horse books and dreaming of the day she would get a horse of her own.

"I remember clomping around in my mother's old English riding boots when they came well up over my knees," said Sanderson. "I read *King of the Wind, The Black Stallion, My Friend Flicka* and every other horse book I could find, but we didn't live in horse country."

Sanderson finally realized her dream when, with their three young children, she and her husband, Tom, moved to Norco, a horse-crazy town in southern California. They bought a nice little blood bay riding mare, who turned out to be in foal. When a palomino filly, Surprise, was born, they fell happily head over heels into the world of horses.

As a professional journalist and photographer, Sanderson began to write for horse magazines in the 1970s. She published over 300 articles in such nationally known magazines as *The Western Horseman, Horse of Course,* and *The Appaloosa Journal.* After retiring from *The Riverside Press-Enterprise,* she published her first book, *Summer of the Spanish Horse.* Readers of that story will find some old friends and familiar places in *Summer of the Spotted Horse.*